NOW YOU ARE TOLD

A Collection of True Tales from My Yesteryears

Bill Neal

ISBN 978-1-64468-051-3 (Paperback)
ISBN 978-1-64468-052-0 (Hardcover)
ISBN 978-1-64468-053-7 (Digital)

First Edition

Covenant Books, Inc.
11661 Hwy 707
Murrells Inlet, SC 29576
www.covenantbooks.com

For my grandfather, William Overton Neal Jr.,
"Uncle Billy"
Oklahoma Territory Cowboy and West Texas Pioneer Rancher

Other Books by Bill Neal

Local History Books

- *The Last Frontier: The Story of Hardeman County* (Eakin Press, 1965, reprint 1996)
- *Our Stories: Legend of the Mounds: The Medicine Mound Settlers' Community Scrapbook* (Nortex Press, 1997)

Historical Nonfiction Books

- *Getting Away with Murder on the Texas Frontier: Notorious Killings & Celebrated Trials* (Texas Tech University Press, 2006)
- *From Guns to Gavels: How Justice Grew Up in the Outlaw West* (Texas Tech University Press, 2008)
- *Sex Murder and the Unwritten Law: Courting Judicial Mayhem, Texas Style* (Texas Tech University Press, 2009, American Liberty & Justice Series book)
- *Vengeance Is Mine: The Scandalous Love Triangle that Triggered the Boyce-Sneed Feud* (University of North Texas Press, 2011, A. C. Greene Series #11)
- *Skullduggery, Secrets, and Murders: The 1894 Wells Fargo Scam That Backfired* (Texas Tech University Press, 2015, American Liberty & Justice Series)
- *Death on the Lonely Llano Estacado: The Assassination of J. W. Jarrott, a Forgotten Hero* (University of North Texas Press, 2017, A. C. Greene Series #17)

"The time has come," the Walrus said,
"To talk of many things:
Of shoes, and ships, and sealing wax,
Of cabbages and kings,
And why the sea is boiling hot—
And whether pigs have wings."

—Lewis Carroll,
Through the Looking-Glass

CONTENTS

LIST OF FIGURES

FOREWORD

My best friend and former law partner, Bill Neal, just came out with another book. His many nonfiction historical books(often with a humorous twist) generally cover West Texas, western Oklahoma, and eastern New Mexico, 1875–1930. He alternates between Texas Tech and the University of North Texas as publishers with many of his books also available from Amazon. All of his books are what I would call winners, but my two favorites are *Death on the Lonely Llano Estacado: The Assassination of J. W. Jarrott, a Forgotten Hero* (a whodunit) and *From Guns to Gavels: How Justice Grew Up in the Outlaw West,* a collection of infamous shootouts and trials. You will be intrigued!

Bill is a native of Medicine Mound, Texas, and before his retirement in 2004 was considered one of the very best trial attorneys in northwest Texas. The boy from Medicine Mound almost got kicked out of Hardin-Simmons University in Abilene on a few occasions with poker legend Doyle Brunson as a roommate. He later graduated number one from the University of Texas law school in Austin. Then he served a year as a briefing attorney for the Texas Supreme Court.

Bill once was invited to appear on *The Phil Donahue Show*, but fearing a few snakes in the grass, he declined.

Besides having been a trial lawyer for forty years, he is a rancher, author, prankster, oilman, and frequent lecturer, songwriter/musician, and storyteller, as well as a part-time savior of wayward souls! Just an all-around good guy.

Paul Scott
(November 13, 1956–October 14, 2019)

Paul Scott and Bill Neal at the 2017 Medicine Mound Reunion held annually at the Downtown Medicine Mound Museum.

Map: Where It All Happened

Fig. 1. Map showing Texas towns that are included in the stories of this book.

INTRODUCTION

In Granddad's earlier years, he was a cowboy in the wild and untamed Oklahoma Territory. At age twenty-three, he came to Texas and acquired the 6,700-acre Medicine Mound Ranch. He negotiated with a local bank in the county seat town of Quanah for a loan to stake his claim. With that money he purchased the ranch, the horses, the cattle, and the equipment needed and still had some funds left over for operating expenses. When he burrowed a dugout in the banks of the small branch of the Cottonwood Creek there were no houses, no fences, no barns, and no corrals—just land. I never saw him miss a loop.

When Granddad Neal settled on the Medicine Mound Ranch, in 1897, he was unmarried and alone. Two years later he married my grandmother, Alma Baker, daughter of J. F. Baker, another pioneer family nearby; and in 1901 they had the first of four children, my dad, Overton "Boots" Neal.

William "Will" O. Neal Jr. and Alma Baker Neal
on their wedding day, September 24, 1899.

Granddad cleared parts of the ranch for cropland, then built and operated the headquarters and two small houses for ranch hands and their families. He also built a blacksmith shop with a forge where he heated iron red-hot and then hammered it into horseshoes to fit the hooves of each of the ranch horses. In addition, he built many miles of fence by hand from fence posts that he cut from trees. And he kept meticulous records not only of cattle sales and ranch expenses but also of the smallest expenditures. (I later saw one of his daily journals with entries of expenses where he recorded even money spent for treats for his four children. "Overton, 10 cents, candy; Oscar, 5 cents, for soda pop.")

It was a couple of years after World War II before Granddad made the final payment on the ranch mortgage and received a clear title to his land. During that half century he rose every morning well before dawn and worked until dark. On one occasion, a cattle buyer who had come out to the ranch to view the herd and make a bid on the calf crop spent the night at the ranch headquarters. Granddad rousted him up well before daylight. The cattle buyer later remarked, "Well, Uncle Billy, it shore don't take long to spend the night with you."

Over the years, Granddad Neal persevered through numerous adversities: crashing cattle markets, droughts, tick fever quarantines, two world wars, hiring ranch hands, and more. The terrible drought of the 1930s combined with the economic depression of that era was probably the most severe test that he and his family faced. Yet, because the local bankers trusted his honesty and ability with unceasing struggles, Granddad Neal was able to endure the financial and physical hardships of the times. He was able to raise a family of three sons and a daughter, of whom he and his wife, Alma, were very proud.

Windmill with the Medicine Mounds located in the background on the Neal Ranch established in 1898 and sold in 1958. Drawing by Jimmy Clay.

I have so many good memories of Granddad Neal. He often found time to put me aboard his horse with him when I was a toddler and take me on a short jog around the headquarters or occasionally on a fishing trip to the large pond he had constructed near four big mounds on the ranch.

Will Neal and his grandson, author Bill Neal, riding the range on the Neal Ranch. Hardeman County, Texas, circa 1938.

And, every time we met, he always came over, put his hand on top of my head, scruffed it a bit, and said, "Well, Bill-Willum, how be ya?"

I can still hear him.

FLAVOR OF THE TIMES

The Way It Was

Before we begin our story, let me quote you some interesting episodes and newspaper clippings of that day and time to set the stage.

Ranchers vs. the Prairie Dogs

When Granddad Neal acquired the Medicine Mound Ranch in 1897 there was a prairie dog town located on it covering about ten acres. The prairie dogs caused two problems: they ate the grass down to the ground, and they made holes with openings slightly larger than a horse's hoof. If a horse ran across a prairie dog town and stuck his foot in a hole, it would often break his leg. And there was nothing a rancher could do to rehabilitate the horse. Then the rancher would be required to put down the horse.

Therefore, ranchers had a vested interest in eradicating prairie dog towns, and that wasn't easy to do. More than forty years later, in the 1940s, Granddad Neal was still struggling with the problem of how to eradicate the prairie dogs. How he did it I don't recall, but he finally succeeded.

*****

Rabbit Drives
(*Quanah Tribune-Chief,* July 20, 1916)

The people at Medicine Mound united with a number of town men last Friday for a big rabbit drive that netted over eight hundred jackrabbits. The rabbits were shipped to Chicago and netted the hunters ten cents apiece which added to the five-cent bounty for the scalp. That made rabbit hunting pay at least.

About four scores of men and boys took part in the drive, which began from Will Neal's ranch gate early in the morning. The drive started northeast, and went through pastures, and fields of row crops, all thickly infested with jackrabbits. The little animals have lately been coming in by the thousands from the brakes in the south, and are very poor, and have worked great havoc in the cotton patches. One man told us that he had lost twenty acres of cotton by the jackrabbit's ravages.

Even though thousands of rabbits had been killed in that section of the county during the past week, their numbers did not seem to have decreased perceptibly.

Several ladies in buggies laden with provisions showed up at a Hackberry tree on the Moseley Farm for the noon dinner and the way those hungry men sailed into the many good things spread out under that tree was a caution.

Every man reported how many jackrabbits he had killed, and it was found that nearly four hundred had been slaughtered that morning.

Want of ammunition prevented the slaughter from going much over eight hundred. As it was, the drive was a great benefit for the farmers in that neighborhood, while the town men present all felt that they had real sport that day and enjoyed every minute of it.

*****

Rabbit Drive
(*Quanah Tribune-Chief,* January 19, 1918)

Be sure to come to the rabbit drive next week. Everybody should be at his station at 11:30. Everyone is asked to bring a good club along with him as in most drives there has been a shortage of clubs.

*****

Rabbit Scalps for Bounty
(*Quanah Tribune-Chief,* March 9, 1918)

J. H. Hodges brought in 1,016 rabbit scalps and M. O. Fields brought 341 to town for bounty. Several others brought in smaller amounts and swelled the number far past 1500.

*****

Thrift Stamps
(*Quanah Tribune-Chief,* February 2, 1918)

Friday night of this week, prizes of Thrift Stamps aggregating $10.00 will be given to pupils of Big Valley, Old Mounds, Clark, Mount Olive, and Star Valley, for the best essay on "Thrift". The contest will be held at the Medicine Mound School. [During World War I, the US government turned to thrift stamps as one means of financing the war effort while instilling traditional values.]

*****

Crow Blasts
(*Quanah Tribune-Chief,* May 7, 1937)

Two miles northeast of Hackberry [community] was the scene of a crow blast Thursday night under the direction of Austin Aulds of the State Game Department.

Fifteen bombs, each carrying fourteen pounds of machine shop slugs and three sticks of dynamite, were touched off at 10:00 p.m. The bombs were constructed by means of stovepipes extending up into the trees, with the slugs and dynamite placed in the pipes. Each bomb was connected by wires to one switch controlled by a tractor, making it possible for all to be set off at the same time. Approximately one thousand crows were exterminated.

About one hundred spectators witnessed the blasting of these crows.

During the past winter crow blasts ridded nearby Wheeler County of some 200,000 crows in their desperate effort to rid that county of swarms of these pests.

Three years ago, the crows began to drift into Wheeler County, where only a few of the birds had been seen before. Farmers stood guard over their stack lots and took shots at them with shotguns, but still the black clouds swarmed over fields and feed stacks, destroying thousands of dollars of crops.

The roosts of the crows are located during the day while they are feasting on the fields and dynamite bombs are placed in the trees around the roosting place. Then when the birds have settled down for the night, the dynamite is discharged, sending thousands of the pests to their doom.

*****

Roping Jackrabbits

One of Granddad Neal's ranching neighbors was named Jack Vantine. Like other ranchers he was pretty handy with a lariat rope and could rope and catch a runaway steer. But one time he outdid himself. It was on a Saturday afternoon when Jack and several of the men and boys of the Medicine Mound community were pitching dollars and pitching horseshoes or just lollygagging. Jack was playing with his lariat rope when a dog chasing a jackrabbit came right down Main Street of Medicine Mound. He tossed out his rope and caught that jackrabbit as it came by. Of course, that was just like making a hole-in-one in golf—just plain luck—but it made him look like a world champion roper.

CHAPTER 1

Medicine Mound: The Frontier Town That Thrived—Then Almost Died The Night Mrs. Tidmore Torched the Town

The ranch where I grew up was named Medicine Mound Ranch because the largest of four mounds located on the ranch was called Medicine Mound. The mound rose 1,750 feet above the level prairie surrounding it. It acquired that name because the Comanche and Kiowa Indians who had occupied that part of the frontier thought that sick members of their tribes who bathed in a spring at the foot of the mound, ate certain medicinal herbs that grew there, and then slept on top of the mound would be cured of their ailments.

It was about the turn of the twentieth century when American pioneers—mostly farmers and ranchers—began settling on small plots of land in this area. As time went by, a small community they named Medicine Mound began to spring up about three miles east of those four mounds. However, the community really began to grow in 1908, when the Kansas City, Mexico and Orient Railroad began laying down tracks in that area. It became a thriving community with a number of businesses, including a bank, churches, a cotton gin, grain elevators, and a school. But the thriving community was not to last. A great tragedy happened shortly before I was born that would change Medicine Mound forever. Now draw up a chair, sit down, and let me begin telling you my tale.

One of the prominent families of Medicine Mound was the Jim Tidmore family, and if ever there was a story of a whole family who "went to hell in a hand basket," as the old-timers used to describe a destiny of doom on the fast track, it had to be the story of the star-crossed Jim Tidmore family.

For quite a time, everything seemed almost perfect for them. They had it all—premiere social prominence, apparent wealth, a father who was a church deacon, and they were all healthy, popular, intelligent, and physically attractive. It seemed that the sky was the limit.

But just when fate had so generously bestowed its richest favors on the Tidmore family, it turned on them and unleashed an absolute, unmitigated, and focused fury on all five family members. Indeed, misfortune relentlessly ground them down into their own separate—and varied, but equally disastrous—hells.

At the heart of it all is an unsolved case that happened many years ago, in 1933. It was a crime that was never investigated—or even reported to the authorities. Although it almost devastated the Medicine Mound community and caused grievous financial disaster to many, and even though almost everybody in this little community knew about the crime as well as the identity of the perpetrator, still nobody ever said anything about it publicly—until now.

And why? Well, this bizarre yarn, as it unravels, will perhaps give a clue to the answer.

In 1902, Joe C. Tidmore purchased 196 acres of land a couple of miles northeast of Medicine Mound. Joe C. Tidmore was known as "Whistlin' Joe" and he brought with him his wife, Frances Mae Tidmore, and their seven children, including James L. (Jim) Tidmore, who was born February 25, 1877, in Denton County, Texas. Jim, age twenty-five, brought his new wife, Ella whom he apparently married in Denton County prior to moving to Medicine Mound with the whole family.

From the very genesis of the new town, Jim Tidmore played a leading role in the development of the community. Unlike his father, Whistlin' Joe, Jim was not cut out to be a simple farmer. Jim was a hustler and a promoter. In 1909, he established a plat that he named Tidmore's First Addition to the town of Medicine Mound and subdivided it into lots and blocks for sale to the public. This was along the new railroad track and located in the north part of town. Jim built the finest home in the addition and immediately established the J. L. Tidmore Real Estate and Insurance Company. Later, he got into the banking business in Medicine Mound and finally became a prominent cotton buyer in the area. Also, he owned and operated a grocery and general dry goods store.

In addition to his business enterprises, Jim was a social and religious leader. He was ordained as a deacon in the Medicine Mound Baptist Church in1908, when he was only thirty-one years of age. A revealing pair of news stories points up another difference between Jim Tidmore and his father. The local weekly newspaper, *Quanah Tribune-Chief*, once noted that three individuals had been "charged with having been too free with a consignment of wine *belonging to Jim Tidmore*." Baptist deacon Jim Tidmore, obviously stung by the account, lost no time in calling it to the attention of the editor, for the very next edition of the paper contained this "correction." The editor wrote: "Jim Tidmore of Medicine Mound stopped the editor this morning to tell him that it was his father, Joe Tidmore, whose home brew had been swiped, and not his, as we reported last week, which we trust will clear up the atmosphere at the Mounds."

Jim and Ella Tidmore appeared to be the leading citizens of Medicine Mound at that time. They put up quite a front. They dressed well, had a nice home, and later drove a big car that Jim used to travel the area in the course of his cotton-buying business. Jim and Ella had three children: Lena Tidmore, the oldest of the children, was born on January 29, 1899, and later two more handsome and gifted children would join the family. James was born on February 1, 1918, and Dorothy was born July 1, 1919.

The James R. "Jim" Tidmore family. Left to right:
James, Ella, Jim, and Dorothy Tidmore, circa 1925.

However, even before these children were born, the dark clouds of destiny had begun gathering and tragedy had struck this prominent family three times. The first big blow to Ella Tidmore came when her brother accidentally drowned in Lake Kemp. But that was nothing compared to the tragedy that the family suffered in September of 1913. Their daughter, Lena, a gifted and beautiful young lady of fifteen, was dating her nineteen-year-old schoolteacher, Thurman Bellamy, a handsome and popular young man and the son of another very prominent early family, the W. H. Bellamys. The couple was madly in love and happy, as evidenced from the photo of them taken in a horse and buggy on the downtown streets of Medicine Mound.

Thurman Bellamy and Lena Tidmore in Thurman's buggy
in downtown Medicine Mound, Texas, circa 1913.

The tragedy was set in motion when Jim Tidmore forbade his daughter from dating Thurman further. Some speculate it was on account of youth; others say it was because the Tidmores thought they were "better than" other folks. Regardless of Jim's motivations, his directive led to terrible consequences. Lena, unwilling to abide her father's rules, went to Charlie Whittle's drugstore and either stole or somehow persuaded him to sell her a bottle of carbolic acid. She then walked from the drugstore to her home a few blocks away. It was later reported that the railroad section hands observed her drinking something as she walked. In fact, she had drunk all of the carbolic acid on her way home. She opened the front door and died in her mother's arms while expressing her love for Thurman Bellamy.

Earlier in the night, she had mailed Thurman a last love letter stating that life was not worth living without him and that she would wait to meet him in heaven. Lena wrote Thurman that she was going to the "dark river of death," adding, "if I can't live with you on earth, I'll live with you in heaven." Lena died on September 20, 1913.

Big Valley Cemetery tombstone of Lena Tidmore, fifteen-year-old daughter of Jim and Ella Tidmore, who committed suicide in 1913 after her father forbade her from going with her schoolteacher, Thurman Bellamy.

Two years later, yet another tragedy struck. A baby girl was born to Jim and Ella and then died two days later. It would be two more years before James L. Tidmore Jr. was born, soon followed by the birth of Dorothy.

Most of those who recall Ella Tidmore believe that Lena's suicide started her on a long slide into total insanity. Jim's sister and Ella's sister-in-law, Mae Seibert, remembered visiting the Tidmores' home and how difficult it was to get any intelligible conversation out of Ella. She recalled that at times she would find Ella down on the floor playing with some of Lena's toys. Nevertheless, Jim, at least, continued his busy career.

Pictures of Jim and Ella during this period show Jim to be a handsome and apparently robust fellow, well dressed and looking every bit the gentleman and prominent citizen. Ella appears also to have been a handsome and well-dressed woman. She was not only good-looking but known to be a formally educated lady and intelligent. However, she was never much of an outgoing person and only rarely attended any community social events. Her reluctance to participate in community affairs and seeming aloofness may, at least in part, have given rise to the general community consensus of opinion that the Tidmores "put on airs" and viewed themselves as "better than" other folks.

But, if fate had dealt harshly with Ella Tidmore before, it had some equally terrible tricks yet to play on her.

In the mid-1920s it became a common item of gossip in the community that Jim was having a love affair with young Clara Boyd, the unmarried daughter of D. M. Boyd, president of the Medicine Mound bank at that time. She worked in the bank with her father and Jim Tidmore. Clara was nineteen years old and Jim was forty-six—the same age as Clara's father. The Boyd family also lived next door to the Tidmores.

This may have been the blow that pushed Ella over the edge into total madness. From that point, Ella embarked on a most bizarre course of conduct. She was often observed in the wee hours of the night roaming around the community. During the day, she watched the neighbors' comings and goings, and when one would leave, she would often sneak into their house and steal various items, including their groceries—sometimes even pausing to cook their food and then take the cooked meal home with her. But those were some of her lesser eccentricities.

As time went by, Ella developed into a full-blown pyromaniac and a dedicated arsonist, with well poisoning as another sideline.

Some of her earliest efforts in this area were focused on her next-door neighbors, the Boyds. Ruby Jean Boyd, the youngest member of the Boyd family, recalled one night when their family returned home from church to discover a fire ablaze in a storage room in their home. Fortunately, they were able to extinguish it before much damage was done. At the source of the fire, however, there were items that did not belong to the family, indicating that the fire had been set.

A few nights later, the family awakened to the crackling sound of another fire, this one started outside the house at the corner of Clara's bedroom. The family rushed outside and again was able to extinguish the blaze before it got out of control.

Then they made another discovery. Their pet dog was lying dead in the yard. It was learned that it had died of strychnine poisoning and that their water well had been poisoned.

This time the sheriff's office was notified and an investigation begun—only to be shut down at the insistence of D. M. Boyd, for reasons unstated but which may well be imagined. Clara's mother suspected that her husband knew who had set the fires and poisoned the well.

Others recall that, in addition to the dead dog clue, Ella had apparently gotten sloppy with the strychnine and scattered a lot of the white powder around the well and yard, thus alerting the Boyds, who had the good sense not to imbibe of the well water. However, Ella did succeed in poisoning to death nearly all the cats and dogs in the neighborhood at the time.

Although Ella did not again try to burn down the Boyd home, during the next few years she was busy, busy, busy with her torch. She set fire to the drugstore building in downtown Medicine Mound, causing considerable damage. Then, she set fire to a house owned by the Medicine Mound gin, causing minor damage. She scored major damage, however, when she torched the grain elevator. Again, there was no question but that it was arson, as a pair of Jim Tidmore's pants with his laundry mark on them was found at the point of the fire's origin.

This fire apparently occurred shortly after the unexpected death of Jim Tidmore on January 27, 1931. Jim had been admitted to the hospital for an appendectomy and was recovering when suddenly he contracted pneumonia and died within a few days. His death was another shocking blow that plunged Ella yet deeper into mental chaos.

The *Quanah Tribune-Chief*, in noting the passing of Jim Tidmore, stated that this pioneer resident of Medicine Mound was known throughout this area of the state as a very prominent businessman.

Despite appearances, it turned out that Jim Tidmore was almost broke when he died. He had no life insurance to provide for his wife and two children. Jim Tidmore's total estate amounted to less than five thousand dollars. He left no will either, which meant his two minor children would inherit most of his estate. Ella had to take out a guardianship for the two children and periodically petition the county court for meager funds to support herself and them. At the time of Jim's death, James was fourteen and Dorothy was thirteen.

Dorothy and James were both gifted students. They made almost all A's in their school subjects. James was handsome and Dorothy was one of the prettiest, if not the prettiest, girl in school.

But Ella's children's successes could not wash away Jim's death or the grinding poverty, and her preoccupation with fire only increased over time. Her biggest torch job was yet to come. And in this one, she succeeded grandly. On a windy March night, in the wee hours of the morning, Ella set fire to the whole downtown section of Medicine Mound. She started at the south end (the wind being from the south that night) and managed to burn down every business building.

Everybody in town knew who did it.

In fact, while the conflagration was at its height, Ella Tidmore was observed by her neighbors standing out in her front yard, laughing hysterically.

*****

Torching the entire town and poisoning the neighbors' water wells were not the only crimes Ella committed. Andy Hale was a neighbor of the Tidmores, and just across the railroad tracks from the Tidmore residence, he had a maize patch. It was getting on late in the summer and the maize had headed out. Andy anticipated making a fine harvest. However, he began noticing that somebody was sneaking into his maize patch at night and beheading his maize stalks, taking the heads with them. Therefore, one moonlit night, he decided that he would hide in the patch, catch the villain, and bring him to book. So he did. And sure enough, about midnight, he heard the culprit coming through the patch whacking off the heads of his maize and sacking them up. Andy Hale crept forward with his shotgun primed and ready and very quietly slipped up behind the maize thief. He could see his prey clearly in the bright moonlight. But just as he was about to throw down on the culprit, she turned her head, and lo and behold, he saw that it was none other than Ella Tidmore. Being no fool, and not caring to have his home burned or his well poisoned, Andy Hale, very carefully, retreated without a sound, never calling Ella's attention to his presence. To hell with the maize crop.

Later, Ella lived with first one and then another of Jim Tidmore's siblings until none of them would put up with her anymore. In 1951, Dorothy moved to Hollywood, California, and Ella soon followed her. When Ella died, neither James nor Dorothy nor any other relative claimed her body, and she was buried in a pauper's grave at the expense of the state of California.

So ends the sad saga of Jim and Ella Tidmore and their three children.

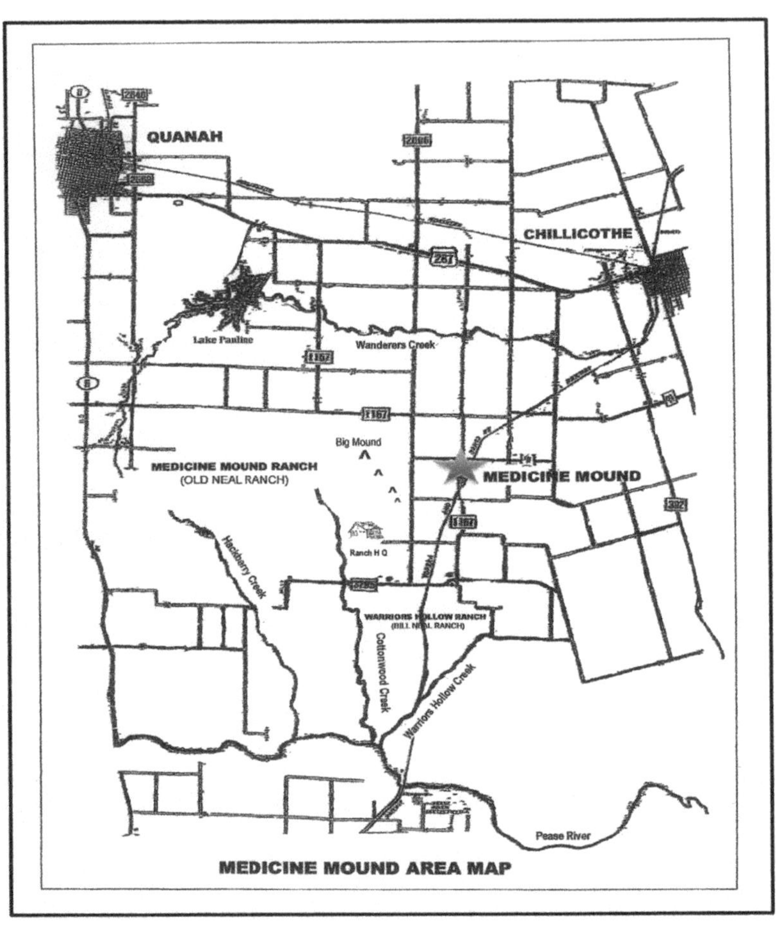

Map: Medicine Mound Area

Fig. 2. Detailed map of the Medicine Mound area, including the Old Neal Ranch and the Warriors Hollow Ranch, which I owned for many years.

CHAPTER 2

Riding in the Feed Wagon with Granddad Neal What a Great Memory It Was

I was only four years old that snowy winter morning in 1940. The scene: the Neal Ranch near the Medicine Mound community in Hardeman County, Texas. Our herd of cattle had to be fed. We left the ranch headquarters and rode for several miles to the feed ground in the pasture. I was riding on the seat of our feed wagon being pulled by a team of two mules to the center of our pasture where we fed our cow herd every other morning during the winter. We fed them a protein supplement called cottonseed cake, and the wagon was loaded with it. While the white strands of cotton were used to make fabric for clothing and other textiles, the little black seeds below the white bolls contained a rich protein that, when crushed, was used to feed livestock. The cottonseed cake was shaped like a very large round cigar about three inches long. Cattle loved to eat that cottonseed cake as much as us kids loved a candy bar, and it provided the needed protein during the winter months when the prairie grass loses much of its protein content.

That morning we had a load of cottonseed cake in hundred-pound sacks ready to distribute to the cows when they arrived at the feed ground. We had about 350 head of cows plus about twenty bulls. As we started getting close to the feed grounds, Granddad began a loud bellowing call that the cattle knew to be a call for the feed. Can't exactly describe it but it sounded something like a cross between a yell and a yodel. That started the cattle moving toward the feed grounds at a fast trot.

William Overton "Boots" Neal III riding Old Silver and shoving cattle to the feed ground on the Neal Ranch in the winter of 1940.

Meanwhile, my dad, Boots Neal, was astride a horse riding the outer boundary of the pasture shoving the cows he came across toward the center of the pasture so they could hear Granddad's call. When the herd reached us, Dad and Granddad would begin quickly spreading the cottonseed cake around on the ground and trying to avoid getting trampled by the cattle.

Cattle gathered at the feed ground on the old Neal Ranch in the winter of 1940.

I remember feeling so grown up and important to be seated beside my granddad while we were doing such important and grown-up work.

CHAPTER 3

Pearl Harbor Day Memories And Air-Raid Drills in Grammar School

Pearl Harbor Day: December 7, 1941. Even though I was only five years old—two months shy of my sixth birthday—I have a vivid memory indelibly etched in my mind of that day. Winter was approaching, but nonetheless the day was pleasant, the temperature was mild, the sun was shining, and there was no wind. It was a beautiful Sunday.

That Sunday, two couples from Quanah—close family friends—drove fifteen miles southeast to our ranch in Medicine Mound to spend an enjoyable day with us. After lunch we all saddled our horses and went for a ride—the grown-ups talking, visiting, and just soaking up a beautiful afternoon, and me, tagging along behind on my Shetland pony. In the late afternoon, we drifted back to the headquarters, unsaddled the ponies in the barn, and walked back to our home. Everybody was still chatting and joking. Totally relaxed.

The Neal Ranch headquarters was my childhood home located at the end of the Neal Ranch road. The house was built right before the turn of the nineteenth century by Grandfather Neal shortly after his marriage to Alma Baker. It had three bedrooms and a bathroom but was without electricity or phone service.

Then, just before sundown, somebody turned on the radio. The good times abruptly ended. None of the grown-ups spoke a word while they listened, stunned speechless by the unbelievable news. A swarm of Japanese airplanes had unexpectedly bombed Pearl Harbor in Hawaii! The radio newsmen were hysterical. First reports were fragmentary. Then awesome details of the attack began to trickle in bit by bit. Damage was catastrophic. US battleships had been sunk, taking hundreds of sailors down with them! Other sailors had been shot and killed by strafing machine-gun fire from enemy planes while still on the ship decks. Our airplanes were caught by surprise and never got off the ground. Blasted and destroyed. Many casualties. No telling how many. Undoubtedly in the thousands!

Our visitors that Sunday night stayed glued to the radio with my dad and mom until the early morning hours. I remember them being shocked and dazed. I didn't know exactly what had happened, but I knew whatever it was, it was something terrible. Awful. The most awful thing I had ever heard. So terrible that it had overwhelmed all the grown-ups.

The next thing I remember hearing on our radio was President Roosevelt saying, "December 7, 1941, is a date which will live in infamy."

Our nation was at war!

For the next four years there was not very much laughter or good times. Every night we were riveted to our radio, listening to the war news, and the war news in those first three years was seldom good. Would the Japanese or the Germans invade us? Would we lose the war? Would those foreign devils take over and enslave us? Take my mom and dad away? Kill us all?

I recall in the spring of 1942, just a few months after the bombing, taking a shovel and going out behind our barn and digging a deep foxhole in which to hide if the radio warned us that the enemy was invading our shores.

Meanwhile, we all were willing to do whatever we could to help our soldiers and sailors, including doing without some things that we really needed. Gasoline, tires, meat, sugar, shoes, and other items were available only in limited quantities. Each family had to have ration stamps to buy these goods. People grew "victory gardens" and shared the vegetables with neighbors. Our nation was united, and everybody wanted to be a part of preserving our freedom, our America.

Many neighbors and family members enlisted or were drafted to fight the war, and soon we began receiving news that some of our soldiers had been wounded or killed or were missing in action. One neighbor boy, Norman Tidwell, who had not yet reached his twentieth birthday, was killed. Our rural mail carrier got the War Department letter addressed to Norman's parents, a letter that contained the heart-breaking news. Somehow, the mail carrier became aware of—or guessed at—the contents of the letter and arranged for several neighbors to be present at the Tidwell farm when he delivered that dreadful missive.

That first fall, the fall of 1942, I started first grade at our tiny community school in Medicine Mound with only about a dozen of us scholars in the first grade. We held air-raid drills, and it was very serious business for one and all. When the air-raid warning bell sounded, we all dutifully and quietly rose from our desks, lined up, and, on signal, silently marched to the basement. There, in darkness and silence, we anxiously awaited the "all-clear" signal, meanwhile hoping desperately that it really was only a drill and not the real thing. The minutes seemed to drag on for hours.

Medicine Mound Grammar School rhythm band directed by author Bill Neal on far left, circa 1942.

Years later, long after the war was over, I reflected back with a bit of humor on how seriously we all took those air-raid drills at our little remote country school. I imagined a scenario that was probably taking place over in Tokyo while we Medicine Mound Grammar School kids hunkered silently in our dark basement. I imagined this: Japanese War Minister Hideki Tojo strides into his headquarters, and all present snap to attention. Then Tojo barks his orders: "Send secret code message to Admiral Yamamoto: All planes to be fully armed, fueled, and in the air by six hundred hours tomorrow. Strike and annihilate that damned grammar school over at Medicine Mound, Texas. Take no prisoners!"

By the time I imagined that scenario, however, we were once again enjoying some sunny and peaceful Sunday afternoons on our ranch—thanks to our soldiers and sailors and all others who had sacrificed so much.

CHAPTER 4

A Cotton-Patch Economics Lesson And a Halloween Like No Other

In the fall of 1942, I learned a valuable lesson in economics—a lesson that wasn't taught in school. That class opened in a cotton patch. Although cattle ranching was our primary pursuit, Dad also planted about forty acres of cultivated land in cotton. The cotton harvest usually began in the middle or last part of September and lasted for six weeks or so. Most of our neighbors were small farmers, and cotton was their main crop. Therefore, when cotton harvest rolled around there was no time for frivolity—it was a daylight-to-dark grind to get the crop to the local gin. In those days, there was no such thing as a mechanical cotton picker. As a result, it was the custom in our community for school to be recessed for about a month to allow students to help with their family's cotton harvest.

Dad gave me a cotton sack, and like the other kids, I dragged it up and down the rows "pullin' bolls"—a most hot, dusty, and unromantic task. But, hey, I was making good money! Since I was a first grader, I didn't have to pick all day; after about four hours Dad excused me. Like the other pickers, Dad paid me two cents per pound. Every evening we weighed our cotton-filled sacks in the field and marked down our take. By late October, I figured I was nearly rich, having acquired a fortune amounting to about ten dollars.

Then came the annual community Halloween party held in the school gymnasium. There were all kinds of booths to enter and games to play and prizes to be won. How exciting! I took my ten-dollar fortune and joined in the games with gusto, and I won a few prizes, which, at the moment, seemed so grand. However, after a couple of hours, my fortune had dried up, and those prizes suddenly seemed kind of dinky and tawdry. A sobering thought then occurred: I vividly recalled all those hours and days of dragging that cussed cotton sack on sore knees and with an aching back, and now my fortune was all gone—all gone! Gone so quickly and for so little—only a few trinkets that I'd stick in the closet and soon forget about. This was the lesson I learned from that episode: It sure takes a lot more time and is a lot harder to earn a dollar than it does to spend it.

Today I am the owner of a small ranch. It is located in the shadow of those "medicine mounds," and it is paid for. And no vultures of foreclosure circle overhead.

And I never, ever have planted one damn stalk of cotton on my land.

CHAPTER 5

Erasing Mistakes with the Undertaker: A Grammar School Memory

Each year at the beginning of the school term when I was attending grammar school at Medicine Mound, a kindly gentleman showed up at our classroom without any previous announcement. He was not a schoolteacher or anyone affiliated with the school, but strangely enough when our teacher saw him enter the room she immediately stood and invited him to speak to the class.

He was a smiling and pleasant man and he brought each of us a gift and presented it to us individually. The gift he presented to us was a large yellow pencil with an eraser on the end. He then began to speak for a few moments. I recall him calling our attention to the eraser at the end of the pencil. He informed us that the eraser was there for a very important purpose. "When you make a mistake, you can erase it and start over again. Everybody makes mistakes, whether you're a child or a grown-up. But the important thing to remember after you make a mistake, you need to pick yourself up, dust yourself off, and start all over again." The pencil he gave each of us was inscribed with the name of his business, the W. H. Smith Funeral Home of Quanah, Texas.

There were many times over the years when I made mistakes and was reminded of Mr. Smith's statement that mistakes can be corrected. I later realized that Mr. Smith was welcomed in every grammar school in the entire county, and at that time there were approximately thirty grammar schools in Hardeman County.

But giving pencils to us grade school children and offering a brief teaching about the importance of overcoming our mistakes I later learned was not the only helpful presentation that Mr. Smith made to all the surrounding communities in the county. In addition to free pencils, he also acquired hand fans, which he distributed to all the different community churches to be used for gatherings. Bear in mind that there was no air-conditioning in those days. During the summer months when gatherings were held, the heat was stifling, and everyone, adults and children, made use of those fans throughout the occasion.

CHAPTER 6

Me and Sambo
A Lesson in Life I Never Forgot

Every fall, the rural counties in our West Texas area hold a livestock show where children from grade school through high school can present the prize livestock they have raised and trained. It is a big event in small rural areas for every youngster, and the winner of the contest receives "best in show" honors.

There are different divisions for bulls, cows, heifers and steers, pigs, chickens, rabbits, and seemingly every other animal one could raise. The most coveted title is usually for the best steer in the show. Younger kids are members of the county 4-H clubs, while older students in high school are members of the FFA (Future Farmers of America) clubs.

When I was about eight years old, my prize animal was a black Angus steer I had raised from the time he was weaned from his mother on our ranch just south of Quanah. I was an only child, and animals from horses down to chickens were a big part of my life. I had fed and nurtured that black Angus steer, which I named Sambo, his whole life. Kept him in a small pasture near our barn and fed, petted, and pampered him. Every afternoon I would fill my pockets with cottonseed cake and go out to see Sambo. When he saw me enter the gate to the barnyard, he would trot over and enjoy his treats. Then I would take a currycomb and rub him down, grooming his body hair while talking to him, complimenting him, and bringing him up to date on events of the day. It was a daily ritual that we both enjoyed.

There were no other families with children for playmates living within about five miles of our ranch home. Sambo became my best friend, my brother as it were.

As fall came upon us, it was time for the annual Hardeman County Livestock Show to be held in Quanah. There I would get to display my brother, Sambo, in the highest-regarded class in show. I had washed, curried, and prepared Sambo for the big event. Dad even bought a brand-new leather halter for him with a short rope attached, which I held to lead him around the show ring for the judges to appraise his rank among all the other steers in the show that year; I believe it was 1944. After much anticipation, the judge who was in the show ring sizing up the quality of the animals announced the results: I didn't win the grand champion steer award, but I was close. I won second place. The judge announced that if Sambo had weighed only a few pounds more, he would have won first place. He then pinned the second-place ribbon on his halter—a ribbon that I still have in my childhood memorabilia.

Bill Neal, age 8 and his show calf, Sambo, at the annual Hardeman County Livestock Show in 1944.

I was so proud I nearly busted. I felt like I had won the world championship. Sambo and I strutted around the show ring a few more times, taking applause from the spectators. I could hardly wait to start bragging on him.

The next day, there was to be a sale for all the kids to sell their show animals. It was to be held at the county's auction barn, where a large group of men would bid on each animal in the show. The highest bidder would take home the prize animal.

I was still excited about Sambo's win. I led Sambo into the bidding ring below the spectators and bidders, where all of the animals would be presented. At the center of the ring, the auctioneer began taking bids and encouraged bidders to raise the bids until he finally announced the winner and the total amount of the winning bid. Then the animal was led out of the ring.

I was ecstatic when I led Sambo into the bidder's ring and heard the announcer praise the quality of Sambo and encourage bids. Meanwhile, all those folks were bidding on Sambo, and I was busting with pride, as I led Sambo back and forth in front of the crowd. When the bidding was finally over, I led Sambo out of the ring.

Then something happened to me. Hit me like a bolt of lightning!

Sambo was not mine anymore! Worse yet, the man who now owned Sambo was going to take him where he would be killed and then made into hamburger and sold in grocery stores!

I looked down at Sambo, who was still ambling along behind me enjoying his time in the limelight. Still trusting me, his dear friend, to take care of him.

What a traitor I had become!

I handed Sambo over to his new owner, feeling myself a modern-day Judas Iscariot.

I returned to our desolate ranch home that evening sad and alone. It was the saddest lesson I ever learned.

CHAPTER 7

My BB Gun Adventures Captured and Disarmed

On my fifth birthday, my dad bought me a BB gun. Now, that was a present that surprised and thrilled me. On our ranch outside of Medicine Mound, hunting and fishing were and had always been the favorite sports of the men there. I couldn't wait to try that BB gun.

Two or three months later, I succeeded in bagging my first game with my new BB gun. It was a large dove. I was so excited to show off my first conquest to my friends in town. Shortly after I shot the thing, I stuffed the dead dove behind the passenger seat so later I could get it out and show it to my friend, James Roy Barnes, right away. I knew that on Saturday, we would drive to Medicine Mound for supplies, and my mother would stop by the Barnes home to visit with James Roy's mother. So there the dove stayed behind the passenger's seat for just about a week until Mom and I drove to Medicine Mound.

After we returned home, I just couldn't bring myself to throw away my prize bird. I continued to keep it behind the passenger's seat of the car. We didn't go back to town for another week, and when my mother got into the car to make her weekly trip to Medicine Mound, she paused before starting the car and sniffed the air. Looking around she said, "What is that awful stench?" I just kept silent, not wanting to admit that I knew where that stench was coming from. After about a five-minute search, my mom discovered my prize trophy stuffed behind the passenger's seat. She then proceeded to throw away my dead bird. I was instructed not to hide anymore hunting trophies in our car.

I did, however, continue to develop my hunting skills with my new BB gun every day. And birds were my main targets.

Years later, when I was in the fifth grade, my mom got a job teaching in grade school in the nearby town of Crowell, Texas, which was about twenty miles from our ranch. She rented a little house where we stayed during the week and Dad stayed at the ranch to work. We would travel back to the ranch on the weekends.

While living in the little house in Crowell, I, of course, took my BB gun with me. I was thrilled to discover that a wealthy lady lived down the street a block away, and I noticed that she had a very large yard with many trees in it. And there were many birds in those trees. I couldn't wait to begin harvesting the prey in my newfound hunting spot. But the wealthy lady who owned that forest left her house one day and saw me shooting the birds in her trees. I was given a stern lecture, and she took my BB gun and marched me down the street to our house…where she gave my mom and me quite a talking-to for attacking the birds in her bird sanctuary. My mother proceeded to take my BB gun and lock it in the closet.

The following weekend, Mom took my BB gun back to our ranch home, where it stayed. I had to find another sport and soon I was playing games like touch football and kick-the-can with my new school friends.

CHAPTER 8

Practicing to Be a Cowboy
Me and Annabelle Bringing Up the Drags

I was raised on Granddad Neal's Medicine Mound Ranch. It was a cow and calf operation consisting of four hundred or five hundred head of mother cows and their annual calf crop.

Whenever we moved the entire herd, Dad and Granddad Neal would ride along each side of the cattle herd and keep them pointed in the right direction. When I reached ten or twelve years old, I was assigned duty of "ridin' the drags." That is, riding behind the herd and keeping them together and not allowing any of the animals to drop out. My mount and dear companion of those years was a trusty mule—her name was Annabelle. She might not have been as picturesque as a quarter horse, and she certainly was not likely to finish first in the Kentucky Derby. But Annabelle and I were more than enough to "ride the drags" of the herd and keep them all together and headed in the right direction.

Bill Neal on Annabelle on the Neal Ranch owned by Bill's grandfather William Overton "Uncle Billy" Neal and his father Overton "Boots" Neal south of Quanah in Hardeman County, Texas. Annabelle was a mule on the ranch that Bill rode to bring up the drags during cattle drives.

Annabelle was reliable, sure-footed, and easy to catch and saddle. The drags of the herd usually consisted of mother cows with baby calves. To entertain myself and develop my roping skills like a real range cowboy, I practiced roping the calves that were trailing along with their mothers. First, I tied one end of my rope to the saddle horn. Then, to facilitate my roping skills, I fashioned a loop at the other end of my rope large enough to loop a calf but allow the calf to step through the loop and escape. This allowed me to continue my roping practice without being required to dismount Annabelle after each catch to release the calf. This knotted loop was not big enough for a grown cow to pass through and escape and that caused a problem one day.

Usually the mother cows kept plodding along, passing like the rest of the cows toward the leaders of the cowherd. Sometimes, however, one of the cows in the drag would become annoyed at one of the other cows and would suddenly, without warning, turn and butt the cow on her left or her right.

That's what happened on this drive. I had just picked out her baby as my roping target and cast my loop for her calf when a momma cow wheeled her head to the left to butt another mother cow. Result: My loop sailed just right to catch the mother cow instead of her calf. Suddenly, Annabelle and I were jerked sideways with a big Hereford mother cow that outweighed both of us and we were headed for a big mesquite tree thicket beside the herd's path. Annabelle and I became tangled up with the cow in the mesquite thicket.

Fortunately, my dad heard the commotion and headed back to untangle me, Annabelle, and the mother cow; and without anybody getting seriously injured by the thorns on the trees in that mesquite thicket. But a few minor scratches didn't interrupt my roping practice.

*****

A few years later, when I was in high school, my roping practice was done for another ranch job. It was a time when blowflies were targeting bloody wounds on cattle. Blowflies will use the bloody wound to lay eggs that develop into screwworms, which if not promptly treated will eat the cow's flesh and eventually kill the animal. During calving time in the spring and summer, my job was to ride our pastures, and when I spotted a newborn calf, I roped and caught it and smeared some black tar substance over the bloody umbilical cord to prevent blowflies from laying their eggs.

I was riding Ole Smokey during this time. He might not have been as calm and sure-footed as Annabelle, but he was faster to catch up with a burst of speed between mesquite thickets to allow me to catch the calf and doctor it. I enjoyed the chase and the roping practice.

One time during the 1970s, I encountered a much more complicated screwworm doctoring case. After catching and doctoring the newborn calf, I noticed that the calf's mother was lying on the ground in a heap of trouble. A sizeable portion of the afterbirth was still dangling from her vagina and blowflies had already begun attacking. But roping her in the pasture would not get the job done. I needed help. I rode back to our ranch headquarters and found our best ranch cowboy, Wayne Weatherred, and explained the problem. We rode back to the mother cow, hoping to drive her back to the ranch corrals so we could get her into a squeeze chute and doctor her. But the old contrary beast sulked and refused to get up. We had to plan a different strategy. We rode back to headquarters. I left Ole Smokey there and fired up the pickup truck and hooked up the stock trailer. We drove back to the stubborn old momma cow, backed up the stock trailer about ten yards from the cow's head, and stopped and propped open the back gate of the trailer.

I need to stop here and tell you about our stock trailer. It was twenty-five or thirty feet long and had iron sides extending upward about three feet from the floor. From there up it had horizontal metal bars for about another three feet. The top was open.

The plan: Wayne would get on his horse and rope the mother cow as she lay on the ground. Meanwhile, I would play bait, antagonizing the old broad, and when the cow gave chase, Wayne would haul her into the trailer.

The first part of the plan went just fine. With the rear of the stock trailer about thirty feet from the cow's head and the gate open, Wayne mounted his horse and looped his rope around her neck. I was afoot with a sizeable mesquite limb in my hand. I nodded "ready" to Wayne and started running alongside the cow. When I reached her head, I yelled as loud as I could and gave her about three or four whacks on her head, then dropped my club and ran for the backdoor of the trailer. Wayne let go of his rope. According to plan, the old biddy jumped to her feet and started after me. But by the time the enraged beast got to her feet and jumped inside the trailer, I was running toward the front of the stock trailer and had jumped up and caught the horizontal bars.

After Wayne let go of his rope, he dismounted and ran around to the back gate of the trailer and slammed the gate shut. By then I had reached the top bar on the front of the trailer and was up and out. We drove that momma cow back home, put her into the squeeze chute, and cleaned and doctored her. Then we went back and captured her baby and reunited mother and calf.

Neal Ranch Cowboy Wayne Weatherred holding a bobcat he killed on the ranch.

*****

Every year on the ranch we had an annual roundup, which meant rounding up the cattle and counting the cows to make sure none were missing, then working that year's calf crop. Working the calf crop meant Granddad, while still on horseback, would rope one of the yearling calves so we could throw the calf down and hold it while the crew, which included my dad and me, would brand it, castrate it if a male, earmark it, and vaccinate it. Once finished, we would release the calf to the herd. By then Granddad would have another calf roped and ready for us.

Annual Neal Ranch roundup (L-R) Clarence Hanby, Arthur Williams, Frontis Waldrip, Boots Neal, and Bill Neal, circa fall 1956.

At noon on those days, we always looked forward to taking off for an hour or two to enjoy a meal and visit a bit. My mother always prepared the meal and brought it out to the ranch corrals where we all sat on the ground eating and visiting before going back to the corrals and resuming our work.

Dinner on the grounds at the annual Neal Ranch roundup (L-R), Katharine Neal, Bill Neal, Dave McPherson, Boots Neal, Frontis Waldrip, Arthur Williams, Clarence Hamby, and Cotton Stermer, circa 1956.

*****

A few years later, we had switched from Hereford cows to black Angus and Dad had decided we needed Brahma bulls so we could produce "Brangus" cattle.

Accordingly, Dad took off on a Brahma-bull-buying expedition in South Texas. After a few days he returned with—best I recall—about twenty-five or thirty Brahma bulls. We turned the Brahma bulls in with our Angus cowherd.

A couple of weeks later, Dad got a call from one of our neighboring ranchers complaining that one of our Brahma bulls had torn through our fence and was romancing a group of his heifers. He didn't want a bunch of half Brahma calves. Dad assured him we would saddle up and ride over and return the bull to our pasture—a promise that would prove considerably harder to keep than it had been to make.

Dad and I saddled up. I was riding Ole Smokey when we got to the barbed-wire fence dividing our range from the complaining neighbor's pasture. Our Brahma bull was in a mesquite thicket with twenty or so of the neighbor's heifers. We left our gate open and rode about two hundred or three hundred yards into the mesquite thicket, which was in a shallow draw, where Don Juan and his heifer friends were at peace with the world.

Dad and I quietly rode into the bushy draw and slowly eased Don Juan out of the group and started him back toward our pasture and through the gate in the barbed-wire fence. We were nearly to the open gate when Don Juan had second thoughts. He casually stopped, turned around, and slowly headed back for the mesquite draw where his girlfriends were still resting. And he kept right on strutting back to join his girlfriends despite our efforts to ease up closer on both sides and return him to his home range. In fact, he ignored us. We went back again and slowly separated him from his companions. We got him to within about half the length of a football field from our ranch gate when Don Juan again decided that wasn't his plan, and for a second time, he turned around and started back to the mesquite-shaded draw and settled in.

For a third time, we eased him out of his mesquite-shaded draw where his girlfriends were casually at rest and we started him out toward home. He repeated his prior slow stop and began to turn back. I was mad as hell by this time. I had my rope drawn and thought, *You son of a bitch, you're not getting away with that trick this time.* And so I turned Ole Smokey around and spurred him and was getting close enough to teach that Brahma bull a lesson. I was going to rope him, and this time drag him back home through that damn open gate! Just as I was about to teach Don Juan a well-deserved lesson, I heard my dad yell:

"Don't rope that son of a bitch! Don't rope that son of a bitch!"

It was the wisest order that my dad ever gave me.

Ole Smokey and I put on the scales together probably weighed about 1,100 pounds while I'm sure Don Juan would have tipped the scales at about twice that much, at least. Had I caught him, that monstrous Brahma bull would have dragged both of us back into that thorny mesquite thicket and that would have been a bloody disaster.

We ended up going back and slowly and quietly gathering Don Juan and his girlfriends and driving them all back to the headquarters corrals, where we separated Don Juan from his lady friends. The next day, we drove the girlfriends back across our pasture and returned them to that mesquite thicket. We later hired somebody to truck Don Juan back to South Texas, where Dad sold him. I never learned how much money we lost on that transaction, but never brought up the subject!

However, I did learn a valuable lesson in an instant—to listen when my dad gave me an order.

CHAPTER 9

Cows, Catfish, and a Cottonmouth Moccasin Me and Bud Conley in Southeastern Oklahoma

During the 1950s, West Texas suffered a severe drought that included our Medicine Mound Ranch and it lasted until the summer of 1957. By the summer of 1955 we had grazed our pastures to the ground. We were faced with selling off the herd of about four hundred or so cows or finding pasture for them elsewhere. My dad solved this problem by leasing lush pastureland over in southeast Oklahoma just across the Red River and just north of Paris, Texas. The grass was lush and about a foot high. The grass wasn't protein rich like our prairie grasses, but it was sufficient to salvage our herd.

The place Dad leased was along the Kiamichi River—a huge river by West Texas standards—and the only building on the place was an old abandoned shack. No electricity, no running water, no beds or furniture. And that thickly forested eastern Oklahoma territory was still home to outlaws of various stripes, bootleggers, and other miscreants. Dad knew that he would need to send a reliable couple of hands over there to reside and check the herd of cattle daily. So that summer—the summer of 1955, while I was home from college—he sent me and our good friend from Quanah, Bud Conley, to ride herd.

Bud was from a ranching family and was about twenty-five years old. He had been a star football player for Quanah High School and for Texas Tech University, and later he taught school at Quanah High School. Bud and I had a great summer that year in addition to tending to the cattle.

We visited and also enjoyed fishing on the Kiamichi River. One such fishing trip was especially eventful. The river was only about a mile from our cabin, so one afternoon we took our fishing gear and walked over to do some fishing. The fish weren't cooperating with us, however, so just about dusk we gave up and called it a day. I had caught only one fish, a small catfish weighing a pound or less, and had put him on a stringer and staked it to the riverbank about ten yards from where we were fishing. Bud began reeling in our rods and collecting our bait box and tackle boxes. Meanwhile, I walked over to where I had staked the catfish along the shore. It was, as I said, almost dark by now so I untied the stringer and pulled up the fish.

I thought, that catfish is sure bigger than I remembered. I kept pulling up on the stringer, and just about the time I got the fish eye level, Bud came up with his flashlight and shined it on us—me, the catfish, and a very deadly and large water moccasin that had almost swallowed all of my catfish!

It was a sight I shall never forget! I had never before—or since—stared a giant poisonous snake eyeball to eyeball. I let him have my catfish!

I recall that the walk back to the cabin in the dark seemed to take forever. We finally made it and unrolled our bedrolls on the front porch. It was about the longest night I had ever spent. Finally, I went to sleep but didn't sleep very long. Just before sunup, while I was lying on my back, I felt something slowly dragging across my throat. It was long and round. "Another water moccasin!" I immediately concluded. I froze while the snake slowly continued slithering across my neck. At last, it got across my throat.

"Bud!" I muttered. "Flashlight—get the flashlight!" He came over with the flashlight and shined it on the trespasser. It turned out to be a large domestic cat that had dragged its tail across my throat! The cat just sat quietly on the edge of the porch, glancing back at us.

I told Bud I believed I would pass on breakfast that day and headed for the outhouse.

CHAPTER 10

The Excitement of Election Day
A Time before Television

When I was growing up in the 1940s, election night was one of the most exciting times of the year, and especially so in local elections. Large crowds would begin to assemble at the Hardeman County courthouse in Quanah to receive election returns that began coming in during the night and continued into the early morning hours. Unlike today, there were no television reporters to bring up-to-the-minute election results and forecast early winners. As I recall, there were about twenty-five small towns and communities in our county that reported election results to Quanah all through the night. Every small community had a separate voting place, and each of those small communities collected votes from voters who usually lived no farther than five miles from the voting location. Places like Chillicothe and Medicine Mound were larger communities that had voting places, but there were many others such as Acme, Goodlett, Kings High, Big Valley, Farmers Valley, Star Valley, Lake Pauline, Lazare, and others that did not have local voting sites. The most colorful community that I recall was on the south edge of the Red River called Eul Hollow. I loved that name: we always called it "you'll holler."

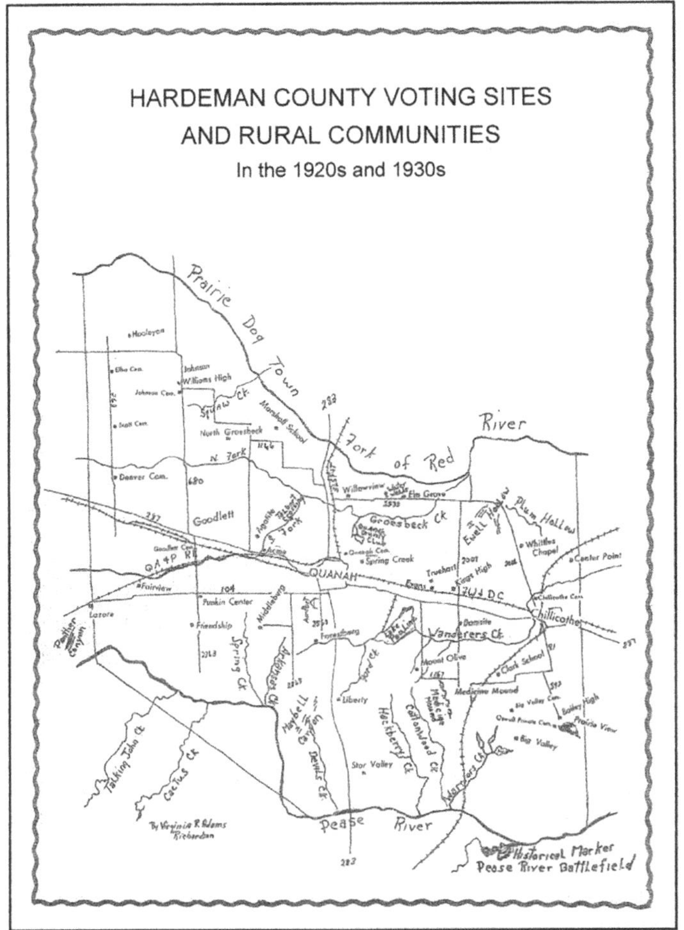

Fig. 3. On election night in the the 1920s and 1930s, crowds congregated at the county courthouse in Quanah and eagerly awaited election returns from the thirty-one communities within Hardeman County. Some of the crowd would stay until the early morning hours for the final returns to arrive and the winners to be announced.

In any event, it took most of the night for all of those election results to trickle into the courthouse in Quanah. Each year, the election officials prepared a large chalkboard listing all the local race positions and candidates in each. As the crowd eagerly waited, the election officials would post the election tally from each community as the voting official arrived with the long-anticipated results.

My dad ran for commissioner of one of the four county precincts (Precinct 2) in Hardeman County. He ran twice against W. F. Caldwell in heated races and won both times. Mr. Caldwell was the incumbent in the first race, which was held in 1932, and my dad won by a slim margin, 139 votes to 113 votes.

IN THE NAME AND BY THE AUTHORITY OF

The State of Texas

TO ALL TO WHOM THESE PRESENTS SHALL COME—GREETING:

KNOW YE, that OVERTON NEAL is hereby commissioned COUNTY COMMISSIONER, PRECINCT NO. TWO, HARDEMAN COUNTY under the laws of the State of Texas with all rights, privileges, and emoluments appertaining to said office.

IN TESTIMONY WHEREOF, I have hereunto signed my name and caused the Seal of State to be affixed at the City of Austin, this the [illegible] day of FEBRUARY, A. D., 193 5.

Governor of Texas.

By the Governor:

Secretary of State.

State of Texas certificate commissioning Overton Neal as county commissioner of Precinct Two of Hardeman County.

While waiting for the individual community reporters to arrive, the crowd visited and speculated on who would win the individual races. In that post-Civil War time, all local political race candidates were Democrats. As late as the 1990s, when I ran for district attorney in a multicounty district, there were still no Republican candidates running for office in West Texas.

I recall one time in the 1990s a young man from one of the northern states moved to Paducah, Texas, and opened a business. He was surprised to find that there were no Republican Party headquarters or Republican candidates on any election ballots in Cottle County. He set about to form a local Republican Party and found little support. He reported his findings while visiting with one of the county residents, who had little enthusiasm for the newcomer's cause. The feller just shrugged and said, "Well, my grandpap was a Democrat. My pap was a Democrat, so I reckon I'll be a Democrat."

The Republican replied, "Well, that doesn't make any sense. What if your grandpap was a horse thief, and your pap was a horse thief? What would that make you?"

After scratching his head, the other feller replied, "Well, I reckon that would make me a Republican."

The presidential election of 1948 was one I will never forget. I was twelve years old, and at that time Grandmother Barnes was living with us. Harry S. Truman had been vice president when Franklin Roosevelt died in office, and he served the rest of Roosevelt's term as president. When election time rolled around, November 2, 1948, the Republicans ran Thomas E. Dewey, a very popular governor of New York, while the Democrats nominated Truman. Little Grandmother Barnes and I were pulling for Truman. She was interested in a lot of things and especially politics.

About nine o'clock, Mom and Dad went to bed, but Grandmother and I stayed up and listened to the presidential election returns on the radio. We didn't have a TV at that time. Early in the night the Republican had a sizeable lead and was predicted to win. Every ten or fifteen minutes the radio announcer would give an election update, and Dewey was ahead. As time went on, however, Truman began picking up more votes. Grandmother and I intently listened to the radio as if it were a close baseball game. By one o'clock in the morning the race had begun to get even tighter. Later that night, *The Chicago Daily Tribune* newspaper printed its November 3, 1948, early morning edition with the now infamous headline across the front page: DEWEY DEFEATS TRUMAN. Meanwhile, Grandmother Barnes and I pulled our chairs up close to the radio and listened intently as the results continued to trickle in. Finally, about four o'clock in the morning, it was announced that Truman had won the election. Grandmother and I jumped up, grabbed each other, and danced a jig around the room.

Our candidate had won!

CHAPTER 11

The Iceman Cometh But Not Always in Time

We didn't get electricity wired to our Medicine Mound ranch house until 1948. Of course, prior to that time we didn't have the benefit of a refrigerator at our home. What we did have, however, was an icebox. The only way my mother could keep food cool and prevent it from spoiling was to store the food in our icebox; and the only way to keep the icebox cool was to place a fresh block of ice in the icebox each week. To accomplish that we had to order blocks of ice from the ice plant located in Quanah. The ice plant's deliveryman made his rounds to rural homes in the area once each week to deliver square blocks weighing either twenty-five or fifty pounds as per the homeowner's order the week before.

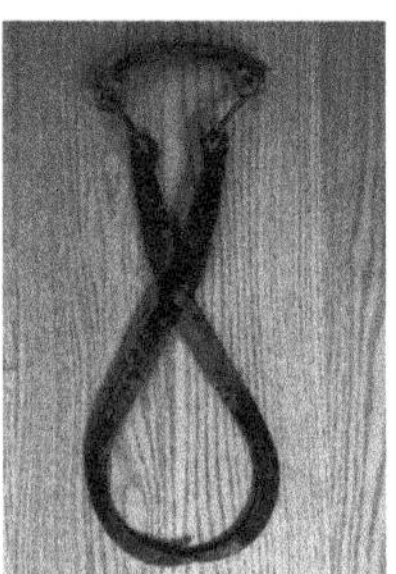

Ice tongs used during my childhood on the Neal Ranch.
Ice tongs were used to carry blocks of ice delivered
weekly from the local icehouse in Quanah, Texas.

When he arrived at the country home he got out his ice tongs and hooked them into the sides of the block of ice and carried it into the home. Iceboxes had hollow walls that were lined with tin or zinc and packed with various insulating materials. The large block of ice was put in a tray or compartment near the top of the box. During the week as the block of ice slowly melted, the water had to be manually discarded from a tray in the icebox.

I remember one summer day when a cattle buyer came to the ranch to see our cattle. After a morning in the pastures, we all went home for lunch. My mother set the table and served us. We all enjoyed a glass of iced tea. Well, one of us did, anyway. The problem was it was toward the end of the week and it was not quite time for the ice deliveryman to deliver a new block of ice. As my mother prepared to serve lunch she chipped a few slivers of ice to put in the tea glasses. However, there was only enough ice left in the icebox for one glass of tea. And, of course, she set that glass of tea in front of our guest, the cattle buyer. The rest of us had to make do with room temperature tea. After lunch, my dad, granddad, and the cattle buyer resumed negotiations for the sale of our cattle. After a lengthy discussion they could not agree on a purchase price and the cattle buyer got in his pickup truck and drove away.

I remember thinking as I watched him drive away, "That son of a bitch drank my glass of cold iced tea and didn't even buy our cattle."

CHAPTER 12

Let There Be Light
Plus, a Mystery: Who Was the Phantom Socket Stuffer?

About sundown one day just after we had unsaddled our horses and left the barn, we stopped to check the western horizon in a forlorn hope of spotting rain clouds. That's when we saw some tall invaders coming toward us over a ridge about four miles to the southwest. The next afternoon there were more of them—still coming at us. Still more the next day.

It wasn't like we hadn't been forewarned. It was just that, well, we'd never seen anything like that out on our remote little ranch in the rough mesquite-flat and cedar-break country along the Pease River in southern Hardeman County, Texas. For years townsfolk had had a lot of fancy things that we never dreamed of having. Electricity, for one.

We had always made do with kerosene lamps, woodstoves, wooden iceboxes, gyp water, and outdoor "johns" (two-holers). Dad had tried a wind-charger to generate homegrown electricity, but with only limited and sporadic success. The damn West Texas wind that bedeviled us so much of the time took a perverse pleasure in calming down about suppertime—just when we needed light. We'd also tried carbide lights, but with only slightly better results. Kerosene lamps were still the standby source of light at night.

Kerosene lanterns were the main source of light in our home when I was growing up on the Neal Ranch, until 1948 when we got electricity.

When they told us one day in 1947 that the Rural Electric Association was going to furnish us with actual electricity just like folks in New York City had enjoyed for years, we gave it a sort of "believe-it-when-we-see-it" shrug. But, by golly, as my mom and my dad and Granddad Neal and my maternal grandmother, Grandmother Barnes, and I maintained a daily back-porch vigil, those REA electric poles kept right on coming straight at us across the prairie until the day finally arrived when they marched right past the barn and set a pole in our backyard. I was eleven years old that day, but to me—and to this day—the word *electricity* still has a magical ring to it that few people today could begin to imagine.

*****

The miracle of electricity took some—actually a lot of—getting used to. When we walked into a room all we had to do was flip a switch and…wow! Lights all over the room! Walk to the next room. Flip another switch and…wow! Again! No wood to chop. No fires to start. No kerosene lamps to light. And when you got ready to sleep, just flip the switch again and…"Good night."

Pure-dee magic.

Adjusting to electricity was a challenge for all of us, but especially for my grandmother Dorothy Barnes, a widow, who had lived with us since her husband and my grandfather, Thomas Milner Barnes, died in 1940. Grandmother Barnes and I were especially close. She was an accomplished artist whose specialty was painting landscapes. Today I have several of her paintings hanging in my home.

Painting by my grandmother, Dorothy Grogard Barnes, of the four mounds during a winter snowstorm at the Neal Ranch as viewed from the windows of our ranch home.

In 1947 Grandmother Barnes was seventy years old, and life had changed suddenly and dramatically from the way she had become accustomed to on the West Texas frontier.

One incident I recall underscored just how dramatic the arrival of electricity in the home was for Grandmother Barnes—an incident that was more than simply illustrative. It was also very amusing.

Maternal grandmother, Dorothy Margarette Grogard Barnes with her sister, Kate. Dorothy appears on the right.

But first let me set the stage. When my dad had our ranch home wired for electricity, he had it done as simply and inexpensively as possible.

We didn't have any fancy electric light fixtures—only one electric cord hanging from the ceiling in the center of each room with one light bulb providing illumination. When one of the light bulbs burned out, Dad would unscrew the bulb and leave the socket vacant until our next trip to town when he would buy a replacement bulb. In our Depression-era mind-set, we thought it too wasteful to spend money on replacement bulbs until we actually had to have one. Anyhow, when that happened, we began to notice that somebody would stuff a rag in the empty socket until a new bulb was secured. But who? And why? Finally, we discovered that the phantom socket stuffer was none other than Grandmother Barnes. Although she was reluctant to discuss the matter, she at last admitted to stuffing the sockets. She was also somewhat reluctant to disclose her motive, but my mother finally pried it out of her. Seeing those empty sockets, it was only logical to assume, at least to Grandmother Barnes, that electricity would be leaking out, and that, in turn, would run up our electric bill. Therefore...

My mother explained that strange as it might seem, no electricity would actually leak out of an empty socket. Grandmother listened and nodded her head. But nevertheless, the next time we had an empty light bulb socket, in a day or two we would come by and notice—sure enough—an old rag was plugging the hole. The phantom socket stuffer had struck again! After all, just because you couldn't *see* electricity, how could you be so darn sure it really wasn't leaking out of that socket?

CHAPTER 13

A True-Life Ranch Romance
Mom Played Cupid for an Unlikely Couple

While cleaning out my dad's old rolltop desk several years ago, I came across a letter addressed to my parents dated January 5, 1951, from Pete Bellamy and his new bride, Juanita Flores Bellamy.

After reading it, I recalled bits and pieces of that unusual romance and my mother's vital role in it. It was a very successful romance and marriage, for Pete and Juanita lived happily together from their wedding in 1951 until Pete's death in 1993.

I have known the Flores family for as long as I can remember. The father, Santos Flores, worked for my granddad and later for my dad off and on for years, and a lot of the time he and his family lived at our Medicine Mound ranch in one of the ranch houses that was a couple hundred yards from our ranch headquarters. Theirs was a large Mexican American family consisting of Santos, his wife, "Charlie," and their eleven children.

Juanita was the oldest, then "Little Santos," Thelma, George (slightly older than me), Pedro (slightly younger), and then "Little Charlie," Lupe, John, Richard, Raymond, and Frankie.

George, Pedro, and I grew up together, roaming around the ranch, hunting and fishing—fishing mainly along the branch of Cottonwood Creek that ran just south of the headquarters.

Juanita and Thelma helped my mother clean house. One day, while so engaged, Juanita and Thelma had one piece of chewing gum they were sharing—a real luxury for them. But instead of dividing it, one would chew the whole thing for a while and then the other got a turn. Mother apparently was not aware of this sharing procedure. Anyhow, just as Mother came into the room, Thelma took the chewing gum out of her mouth and handed it to Juanita, as it was her turn, and Juanita immediately popped it into her mouth and happily started munching away. Mother was shocked. She immediately reprimanded them. However, they missed the point, for instantly Juanita popped it out of her mouth and gave it back to Thelma, who then popped it back into her mouth and began merrily chomping away.

Soon thereafter, Thelma died of a ruptured appendix. It was a real shock to me, as it was my first experience with the death of someone I knew well and was near my age.

Juanita (her real name was Lovita, but everybody called her Juanita) was one of the happiest, most effervescent and enthusiastic people I have ever known. And she was always ready to pitch in and do whatever there was to be done. She was as talkative as Pete Bellamy was taciturn.

When Juanita was about twenty-five years old, she fell in love with Pete. At that time there were very few resident Mexican Americans in the community. Of course, the community was flooded with farm workers who came with the cotton harvest and then were gone. But Juanita never had much opportunity to have any social life of her own. Pete Bellamy was a big, rawboned, silent country boy—sort of Gary Cooperish, but not that handsome. Rather homely, in fact. And, of course, he was Caucasian. The Bellamy family was prominent and had lived in the Medicine Mound community since its earliest settlement. They were not happy about the idea of Pete having any close relationship with Juanita.

Besides the class difference, it was a community taboo in those days for a white man to date a Mexican girl, much less marry one. In fact, if a white man made any advances toward a Mexican woman, his motives were more than suspect.

On the other side of this equation, the couple faced an even more formidable obstacle, and that was Juanita's father, Santos, who was a real tyrant when it came to his family. He was the family dictator, and it didn't make much difference to him what his wife or kids wanted or thought. Santos told them what to do, what not to do, what to think and how to behave, including who was suitable to court and marry. Santos didn't believe in sending his girls to school. Juanita was unable to read or write until after she married Pete and he taught her—but that's getting ahead of the story.

How Pete and Juanita ever got close enough to begin a courtship in those days is a mystery. I don't remember that Santos had a car. And at that time, if you lived five miles out of the small town of Medicine Mound, you were lucky to get to town for groceries and supplies once a week—and never alone. Thinking back, I suspect that it probably happened because my mother took Juanita and two or three of the other older Flores children with her to the Medicine Mound Baptist Church, which the Bellamy family also attended. At any rate, they somehow got together, and romance developed. Santos got wind of it and absolutely forbade Juanita to have anything further to do with Pete. He was a white man, and he had been married before, and he was older. I am sure Santos also suspected that Pete's motives, insofar as this romance was concerned, were less than honorable. Furthermore, Santos wanted to keep Juanita under his control. He didn't want her to marry anybody; he wanted her for himself. This dark secret was one I was not aware of until many years later.

One day, Juanita came to my mother with this problem. She told Mother that she was madly in love with Pete, and she said that Pete was in love with her and that they wanted to get married. At this time, the Flores family was not living on our ranch; they had moved to the Jim Vantine place about two miles west of us across Cottonwood Creek. Mother had worked with Juanita, trying to teach her whatever she could, and had gotten her involved in the Baptist Church—which, I imagine, was not very much to the liking of Santos. Anyway, Mother was the only person to whom Juanita could turn for help.

Katharine Neal dressed for Southern Baptist Women's Missionary Society party, circa 1952.

After hearing Juanita's tearful story, Mother took it under advisement and talked with Dad and then prayed about the matter. Dad, as I recall, was very reluctant to have Mother get involved in this kind of domestic turmoil, for it had all the makings of a very explosive situation. Everybody knew Santos would erupt like a volcano if Juanita ran off with Pete or anybody else, and what he might do was anybody's guess. Everybody also knew that the Bellamy family was much opposed to this match and that most of the community disapproved of mixed-race relationships.

Nevertheless, Mother was not deterred. Her next move was to get Pete off by himself and have a real heart-to-heart talk with him, for I'm sure she shared Santos's concern about how honorable Pete's intentions really were. Pete assured Mother that his intentions were honorable. I do not know what was said, but knowing my mother, he must have undergone quite an interrogation, and I can almost bet he had to swear it all on Mother's Bible. But at last she was convinced, so she set about to facilitate an elopement.

Mother's first requirement was for Pete to get a job somewhere out of this immediate area, and so he did. He got a job at an aircraft factory in the Dallas/Ft. Worth area, rented an apartment, and got everything ready. He then had to swear he would marry Juanita and not see her again until a preacher and marriage license were also present.

At last, he had met all of Mother's requirements, and a date was set. Mother also surreptitiously helped them get a marriage license. She took Juanita to Quanah on the pretext of "visiting a friend in the hospital," got the marriage license, and bought Juanita a suit of clothes.

The day finally came, and by then, even I—who was only fourteen years old and primarily concerned with important stuff, like catching fish and such—was aware of this pending drama and began to get caught up in the excitement. About midnight on that January night, after Santos went to sleep, Juanita got her meager belongings together, put them in a paper grocery bag, and slipped off into the cold darkness—across the cedar breaks and Cottonwood Creek, walking alone to our house where Mother was keeping vigil.

Sometime after midnight, she appeared out of the night, nearly frozen and scared half to death that Santos was on her trail. But apparently, he was still asleep. Mother took her to Vernon, where she caught the train to Dallas, where Pete was waiting for her. The marriage took place in Dallas, and they immediately fled to their apartment—the place being kept a strict secret from everybody except my mother and dad.

I recall that Santos did, in fact, as per all predictions, explode in a paroxysm of rage and tore around the countryside trying to find Pete and Juanita. But the deed was done, and the secret of their whereabouts strictly kept. I am sure he must have suspected that Mother had something to do with it all, and probably a lot, but that was as far as he got. After the dust cleared and Santos had finally accepted the fait accompli, Pete and Juanita often came back to visit us.

After the dust cleared and Santos had finally accepted the fait accompli, Pete and Juanita often came back to visit us. However, as

I recall, it was several years before they dared to return home or let Santos know where they lived.

I have come to realize that my mother was truly courageous, for, in that time, more than seventy years ago, community attitudes, beliefs, and mores were very rigid and there was no tolerance for mixed marriages.

Nevertheless, she did what she believed was right—right for Pete and Juanita—regardless of what Santos might or might not do, and despite the disapproval of Pete's family, and despite the general condemnation of the community.

Looking back upon this incident with the advantage of a lot of years of insight, I see my mother at her best. It took character and it took strength. She rose above her upbringing and above community censure, just to do a simple and good thing that nobody else would ever have considered doing. A thing that meant a lot to two other people—Pete and Juanita.

Mother not only got Juanita out of unnatural bondage to her father, but also gave Juanita the only real chance for happiness that she ever had or would have. Otherwise, she would have been her father's kitchen servant, mistress, and cotton picker for as long as he lived. Afterward, it would have been too late for Juanita. And too late for Pete, for he was, as it turned out, as much a beneficiary of Mother's stand as was Juanita.

The Pete-and-Juanita romance and marriage turned out to be a classic "and they married and lived happily ever after" story. Pete proved to be as solid as a rock and proved he truly loved Juanita as much as Juanita did him. They did not have any natural children, but I recall they adopted three children of the Flores family. (I handled these adoptions for them shortly after I got out of law school.)

This letter from Pete to my parents bears evidence of the kind of folks they were and the success of that union.

LETTER FROM MELZA ("PETE") BELLAMY TO KATHARINE & OVERTON NEAL—
Letter dated Jan. 5, 1951 to "Dear Katharine & Overton" a part of the story: "True Life Ranch Romance" by Bill Neal

2117 [illegible]
Jan 5, 1951

Dear Katherine & Overton
Should have written sooner but as I have changed jobs from Fort Worth and Convair to Dallas & Chance Vaught, I have been pretty busy but I have a job here that I enjoy more not to mention the fact that I make more money and can take better care of Juanita.

Katherine she seems to be happy and has many traits that make for a happy life together. Has her shape fixed up every day, D.M. certainly did a nice job on it for her. Boy did she get [illegible] for washing and ironed shirt to work today! Put knots on my head!

Would it be too much trouble to get Lavita P. Flores a birth certificate? Would like one for her. SANTOS Don't need to know about certificate

Lavita P. Flores
Born - March 14, 1925
at - Del Rio - no record no doctor

Would be better if [illegible] had one for her - don't you think? You know they havn't sent our marriage license back yet.

SANTOS Z. Flores
Born 1901 - May 7
E. Carolota Flores
Born - 1909 - Nov - 30

Katherine, D.M. was telling Juanita when he came from Medicine Mound that "Little [illegible]" was married? She would like to know about this or if he has gone to the army etc. or just about anything you have heard about her family.

All the snow has melted around here. Had a letter from John A. to Minnesota today. They tell us it has been plenty of cold up there.

Juanita wants you to tell her about Alfred and all the folks in her Sunday School class and to tell them all hello for her.

The Churches had a demonstration of the "Salad Master" to night. Been watching their advertisment over "Television". We enjoy television, guess I went wrong to let her look at it, bet I have to buy one now.

Think & talk about you folks each day and be glad when we can all get together. Hope it is soon.

Your grateful friends
Pete & Juanita

Letter dated January 5, 1931, from Melza "Pete" Bellamy to Katharine and Overton Neal.

After Pete retired in 1977 as an aircraft mechanic for LTV in the Dallas/Ft. Worth area, they moved to McCamey, Texas. Pete died on March 8, 1993, in McCamey at age seventy-five, and Juanita continued to live there.

I last saw Juanita in 1994 when she came out to my ranch for a visit—just a couple of miles from the site of the elopement. We recounted those old times.

Juanita Flores Bellamy and author Bill Neal at the Warriors Hollow Ranch near Medicine Mound, Texas, circa 1994.

She recalled that when they first got married, all the clothes she had was what she was wearing. They had two plates, two knives, two forks, and two spoons. They lived in a one-room apartment—had one table and two chairs. Juanita laughingly recalled that, when Mom and Dad came to visit her and Pete shortly after their marriage, she invited them to eat supper. Because of the lack of utensils and chairs, they had to eat in two shifts. First, she served Mom and Dad, and when they were finished eating, she washed the plates and utensils so she and Pete could eat dinner at the table.

CHAPTER 14

Anything Goes—But Not in West Texas "A Glimpse of Stocking Was Looked On as Something Shocking"

My mother was a young, single woman when she moved to the West Texas village of Quanah and began teaching school. She was a young and beautiful at twenty-three years old. In the spring of that same year, my mother, Katharine Barnes, and my dad, Overton Neal, started dating. They soon fell in love and wanted to get married, but at that time women who taught school were required to remain single and retain their virginity. Nevertheless, one Saturday they decided to circumvent that rule. What they did was, they planned to get married but keep it a secret—they eloped. On Valentine's Day, in 1926, together with another young couple, they secretly traveled to the little town of Matador about seventy-five miles west of Quanah and got married just out of range of local gossip. When they returned to Quanah, my mom continued to teach in the Quanah school system and they kept their secret by living separately for the rest of that school year, finally announcing their marriage that summer.

This story illustrates the attitude of folks living in West Texas at that time. It was also evident in the language they used. For instance, instead of saying a woman was pregnant, folks said a woman was "in a family way." Even women's clothing—whether married or unmarried—reflected the public's attitude. Women were expected to wear dresses and skirts that hung to their ankles. Some years later, in 1934, Cole Porter wrote a popular song titled "Anything Goes" that put a humorous twist on the women's dress code of the day. One refrain from that song went as follows:

> In olden days, a glimpse of stocking
> Was looked on as something shocking.
> But now, God knows
> Anything goes.
> Good authors too,
> Who once knew better words,
> Now only use four-letter words writing prose.
> Anything goes.

CHAPTER 15

Family Storytellin'

These are some of my favorite family stories that I heard told by family members while growing up on the ranch.

Arthur and the Buggy Ride

Grandmother Neal had a favorite story she would tell that involved a courtship of sorts back in the horse-and-buggy days. Back about the turn of the twentieth century there was a fellow in the Medicine Mound community, a shy and backward type. (I don't remember his name, so we will call him Arthur.) Not unlike many others brought up in such a rural horse-and-buggy society, his social skills were somewhat limited. Arthur was in his middle twenties before he ever worked up the nerve to ask a girl out. But finally, at church one Sunday he asked one of the young ladies if it might be possible for him to take her on a buggy ride. She agreed to that and they set a time after church the next Sunday afternoon.

At the appointed hour, Arthur duly showed up with his buggy all spic and span and polished and the horse freshly washed, curried, and groomed. Arthur was wearing his best "Sunday-go-to-meeting" clothes and his hair was oiled and slicked down. He called on the young lady and was properly introduced to her parents. They sat around the parlor for a few painfully strained minutes and exchanged a pleasantry or two, and then off they went on their buggy drive.

They were gone for several hours, driving all over the country roads. During all this time, Arthur hardly said a word.

Finally, they came back about five o'clock that evening. Coming down the home lane, he looked over and said, "Well, Miss Ellen, I don't reckon you'll be wanting to see me no more."

She said, "Why, Arthur, what on earth would make you say something like that?"

He looked at her and said, "Oh, you know, I'm just such an old cutup!"

*****

Grandpa Baker and the Ears of Corn

My grandmother Alma Baker Neal's brother, Keatley Baker, was, as they said back then, "smart as a whip." He was also a tireless prankster. Later, he became famous in agricultural experiment work in Marion Junction and Auburn, Alabama. But, growing up, he was forever bedeviling Grandpa Baker and his siblings. One story about Keatley particularly stands out.

He and Grandpa Baker were going to Quanah one cold winter morning in a wagon pulled by a team of mules. Grandpa Baker was driving. As they drove along, Grandpa Baker noticed somebody had spilled some ears of corn along the road. So, Grandpa Baker, being ever a thrifty soul, told Keatley to take over the reins and drive the team. Then he got out and started walking behind the wagon, picking up the ears of corn and throwing them into the wagon bed as they went along. He walked along for a mile or so and kept picking up ears of corn and chucking them into the bed of the wagon. By this time, Grandpa Baker thought he must have recovered a sizeable load of corn. But much to his dismay, when he climbed up on the wagon and looked over the sideboard, there were only about six or seven well-worn ears of corn! Grandpa Baker soon learned that while he was walking along behind the wagon, picking up and chucking those ears of corn in the bed, Keatley was reaching behind him, picking up the ears one at a time, and dropping them to the ground in front of the wagon. Grandpa Baker had been picking up those same few ears of corn over and over and tossing them into the wagon. According to family legend, Grandpa Baker was not overly amused.

*****

Granddad Neal's New Gold Pocket Watch

Sometime in the late 1940s, when Granddad Neal's financial status had improved so much that he was not totally obsessed with making mortgage payments on the ranch, he decided to treat himself to an object that he had wanted all of his life: a pocket watch. He bought one of the highest quality watches on the market at that time. It was a round gold watch with a fob cover and it had a leather strap that attached to the crown. He was so proud of his expensive new gold pocket watch. He carried his new watch in his front pants pocket and tied the leather strap to a belt loop on his pants.

One evening when Granddad came back to the headquarters, it was about sundown. Granddad had read in the Farmer's Almanac that sunset was to occur at 6:15 p.m. Just at sunset he walked to the backdoor, stopped, pulled out his watch, opened the flap, and read the time. It was 6:17 p.m. Granddad was heard muttering to himself, "The son of a bitch went down two minutes too late."

*****

Granddad Neal's Cussin'

Granddad Neal was a hardworking rancher and a man of few words—except on certain occasions. For instance, when we were driving a herd of cattle and one would break out of the herd, Granddad would spur his mount and take in after the old heifer, giving her a good cussin' all the while bringing her back to the herd.

One Sunday night, my parents took me to the local Baptist Church, and the preacher was a real old-time "pulpit-pounder" who recounted the "unforgivable sins," one of which was cussing. That night after we got home and my mom tucked me into bed, she heard me sobbing.

"What on earth is the matter with you, hun?" she asked.

I replied, "Granddad is going straight to hell."

"Why?" Mom asked.

To which I sobbed in reply, "You just ought to have heard him cussin' that old wild heifer that broke out of the herd yesterday."

My mom gently calmed me down and assured me that Granddad was really a good man, and God would forgive him for cussing that old heifer.

*****

"Me First of the Joneses"

One Sunday night when I was about eight or nine years old, my family was invited to a neighbor's house to an ice cream social after church. The family that issued the invitation—the Jones family—had five or six children, the oldest of whom was a red-haired freckle-faced boy about ten or twelve years old named Ben. We all eagerly looked forward to tasting the special treat of homemade ice cream, but first let me explain the process of making homemade ice cream in those days. The women mixed all the necessary ingredients and poured them into the canister of the ice cream freezer. Next, the dasher was inserted into that canister and it was topped with the lid. Now the canister was placed into a larger wooden bucket filled with ice and salt to help freeze the ice cream. Lastly, the crank was placed on top and the turning begun. The process took a long time, or it seemed like a long time to us kids who eagerly awaited a bowl of delicious ice cream.

As the crank became harder and harder to turn, we knew it wouldn't be long and excitement filled the air for us children. Ben, the oldest of the Jones family children, grabbed a spoon, stood beside the ice cream maker, and yelled out, "Me first, me first, me first!"

Ben's mother turned and yelled to Ben: "Mind your manners, we've got company here." With that she backhanded him and knocked him against the wall.

But as he bounced off the wall unfazed he yelled, "Well, me first of the Joneses, me first of the Joneses!"

For years after that night, our family would occasionally recall this story with laughter and use the phrase, "Me first of the Neals, me first of the Neals."

*****

Catching the Phantom Butter Cream Thief

My dad told me that when he was a little boy, they solved a crazy mystery. Who was stealing the cream out of the butter churn when they were gone from home? No one in the family could figure out who was stealing the butter from the churn or how it was being done. To back up a bit, I need to tell you when my dad was growing up, shortly after the turn of the nineteenth century, rural families had milk cows and they made their own butter. Now, let me tell you how a farm family turned milk into butter. They placed the fresh milk into a crock to allow the cream to rise to the top of the milk. Then the wife would put the cream into a butter churn. Butter churns came in several styles and sizes. The one in this story was about three feet tall and filled with cream ready to be churned.

When my dad's family left the home for daily activities, the cream was left in the churn covered with a lid with a small round hole for the handle. The plunger used in the process of making butter had a handle about the diameter of a broomstick. However, the family noticed that if they were gone for several hours, when they returned a large amount of cream left in the butter churn had disappeared. Since no one was home during the disappearance of the cream, the family was puzzled as to what happened to the missing cream. There was one living creature that remained in the house while the family was out and that was the pet raccoon. But if the raccoon was the phantom cream thief, how in the world was he extracting the cream from the butter churn?

This had gone on for quite a while when the family finally decided to solve the mystery of the phantom cream thief. That day before leaving the home, they placed the butter churn near the kitchen window. Then everyone went outside and waited quietly. They could see the churn just inside the kitchen window, and in about fifteen minutes they observed the butter thief in action. The pet raccoon jumped on top of the butter churn and, using his hands, carefully inserted his tail into the hole in the lid of the churn. He slowly extracted his cream-laden tail out of the hole in the lid, and with his two front paws stripped the cream from his tail and proceeded to eat it, repeating the process until he finally had his fill. And that was how the family solved the mystery of the disappearing cream.

Afterwards, when the family left for a day of work, they left the phantom cream thief in another room with the door closed.

*****

The Mystery of the Drunk Ducks

Recalling the raccoon thief story reminds me of another funny story that happened during pioneer days. It was told to me by a friend, Lee Ann Hill. She is a registered nurse and a hard worker and occasionally enjoys telling a funny story or two. But none as outrageous and hilarious as the drunken ducks story that I want to tell you. This is a tale she first heard from her grandmother, Marie Evans Hill. It goes like this:

When Grandmother Hill was a little girl, her family lived on a small farm in a sparsely populated area between Davidson and Fredrick, Oklahoma, in Tillman County. It was a large family with seven children, the parents, and a grandmother. The family was very poor and lived in a shack that sat on a dirt floor. When Grandmother was a little girl, the family had about a dozen ducks. Duck eggs were a part of their daily diet. Every day the ducks were let out early in the morning and allowed to roam the property and forage for food.

One day, the ducks roamed a little farther from home than usual. They went across the road to the neighbor's farm. Now, the neighbor had a little extra business he was conducting on the side. He was making home brew. Apparently, those ducks liked the smell of that brew and proceeded to dive right in and help themselves to the tasty treat. And by the time the drunk ducks staggered back home, they collapsed in the yard, and that's where they lay when the Hill children found them. They ran into the house and reported their discovery to the family. When everyone ran outside and saw the critters, they assumed they had a bunch of dead ducks.

The grandmother was beside herself and said, "Well, let's pluck the feathers. At least we can make some fine feather pillows." With no real beds for sleeping, being able to have new feather pillows was a big deal. So, grandmother and the kids began plucking away. But just as they were about to complete the task the ducks began to sober up. Suddenly the family had a flock of naked ducks roaming the farm! Eventually some of the ducks' feathers grew back, but some ducks never regained their feather covering. The grandmother became so concerned about the naked ducks that she made little simple clothes for them. She didn't want them to get sunburned.

Grandmother Hill enjoyed telling stories all of her life, but one thing made her stories extra funny. She had narcolepsy, and when she laughed her head would drop and she would be asleep for fifteen to twenty seconds, then she would raise her head and go on with her story. Of course, that made her audience giggle even more. Marie Hill died in 2013 at the age of 90.

CHAPTER 16

Jumping into Journalism One Step at a Time

After graduating from high school, I attended college at Hardin-Simmons University in Abilene, Texas, and was majoring in economics. But 'round about my junior year, I got acquainted with A. C. Greene, the journalism teacher. A. C. was an Abilene native and, at that time, a reporter for the daily *Abilene Reporter-News*. He also taught the journalism class each year. I signed up for it. I liked it, so I took a couple more journalism courses and wound up—during my senior year—being editor of the college student newspaper, *The Brand*. A. C. was the man who really stimulated my interest in writing and became my mentor and good friend for the rest of his life. That whetted my appetite for journalism.

In fact, A. C. wrote the foreword to one of my books that focused on the lives and times of the pioneer families I grew up with in the little village of Medicine Mound, Texas.

Our Stories
The Medicine Mound Settlers' Community Scrapbook

Foreword

In 1957 at Hardin-Simmons University in Abilene, I became a teacher for the first time; high school, university or Sunday school. H-SU was in a hurry to fill the job, the previous instructor having resigned just as the new semester began.

I was offered the exalted title: Head of the Journalism Department. I was also the foot. I was the only journalism teacher.

Fortunately for this teaching novice, having had only three hated hours of Education 101, the classes I taught at H-SU happened to have more than the usual percentage of bright young people—and none of them was brighter than Bill Neal. He not only became my best student, he became a good friend, and has remained a friend through all the rough and smooth times that have occurred since.

Bill was both a good writer and a good journalist—not an automatic coupling. As a friend, I helped him overcome one or two major disappointments in his private life, and after graduation, he became almost a member of my family. My late wife, Betty, and I were used to having Bill Neal suddenly show up, lugging along something interesting or good to eat. One freezing, sleeting morning around 2:00 a.m., the doorbell rang and my wife, more awake than I, said, "Who in the world can that be?" or perhaps this H-SU graduate (Class of '49) put it in slightly stronger terms. Opening the front door, she peered into the storm and hurried back to me. "There's something huddled in the yard," she said. I turned on the porch light and recognized the huddled "thing" as Bill. Betty and I got him in the house, stretched him out on a sofa, and covered him with a blanket, as he mumbled about having a wreck. Next morning at breakfast he gave us a few more details. "I rolled my Volkswagen into a very small ball," he said. We asked him what he was doing, "Oh, he said, 'I doubt I was doing much over seventy.'" We never found out how he got to our house.

Bill Neal is forever a writer. He had a go at the family career, ranching, then edited two *Panhandle* weekly newspapers (located 60 miles apart) and was a reporter for the *Abilene Reporter-News* and the *Amarillo Daily[Globe]News* but was always listening and writing about people. People were his history, and I was proud that I supplied the foreword for his first book, *The Last Frontier: The History of Hardeman County*. Even full of pictures and facts, over half the book is about people, individuals, and their families.

Although for the past few decades Bill Neal has been a successful attorney, this, too, has been a form of people-history. And now, in this present volume, *Our Stories: The Medicine Mound Settler's Community Scrapbook*, he returns to his true love. And I am more than willing to give myself credit that my initial effort at communicating knowledge brought a modicum, at least, of colorful response.

A. C. Greene, 1997

*****

Later, in 1958, while I was serving in the Army at Fort Benning, Georgia, my family sold the Medicine Mound Ranch. I had always planned to be a rancher, but now I was faced with a decision of what to do next in my life.

When I returned home that spring from my service in the Army, I began my career as a writer. Carol Koch, editor of the weekly *Quanah Tribune-Chief* newspaper, asked me to compile a written history of Hardeman County, Texas, which was to be included in a special centennial edition of the newspaper that summer. And I did.

When I first started the written history, I didn't realize the magnitude of the task before me. But the more I researched the history of the area, the more intrigued I became. The first area I investigated was the Comanche heritage of the county, which included Chief Quanah Parker, for whom the town of Quanah is named. Quanah Parker was a war leader of the Comanche people. He was the son of Peta Nocona and Cynthia Ann Parker, an Anglo-American who had been captured in 1836, when she was about ten years old, by a Comanche war band that had massacred her family's settlement.

The scope of my investigation into the history of Hardeman County expanded far more than I had anticipated. It included small communities located within the county, the families of early-day settlers, and the life of the communities, which included local businesses, schools, churches, and outstanding historical events that had occurred during the settlement of the county. I also researched and summarized many public records.

Upon completion of the centennial newspaper edition, I realized how much I enjoyed doing historical research, and so a few years later I compiled a book titled *The Last Frontier: The History of Hardeman County, Texas.*

After working that summer for Carol, I moved back to Abilene and was hired to work as a reporter for *The Abilene Reporter-News.* I was assigned the duty of working on the morning edition of the paper. At that time, all daily newspapers in the area printed two editions each day—the morning edition and the evening edition. Back in those days all the reporters had desks in one big room called the newsroom.

At that time, Don Oliver was the sports editor for the paper. Don was quite an egotistical fellow, and one incident I particularly recall involved a student athlete from Abilene Christian College named Bobby Morrow, who had won three gold medals at the 1956 summer Olympic games in Melbourne, Australia; quite an accomplishment for one individual at that time. He had been featured in several magazines including *Sport*, *Sports Illustrated*, and *Time* magazine. Bobby Morrow was a nationwide sensation, appearing in a parade in New York City followed by an appearance on *The Ed Sullivan Show.* I recall an incident that happened at the reporter news with sports desk editor Don

Oliver presiding. Several leading local citizens were gathered around Don Oliver's desk and were excitedly planning a town celebration to honor Bobby Morrow's return to Abilene. The group decided that a famous sports person was needed to lead the celebration.

Don Oliver bragged to the group, "I can get Ben Hogan to come and lead the celebration." When I heard Don Oliver make that remark, I thought to myself, *That will be the day.* Ben Hogan was not only a famous professional golfer of the day, but he had a reputation for refusing to allow any news reporter to interview him. Nevertheless, Don picked up the phone and said to the receptionist downstairs, "Call Ben Hogan in Fort Worth." I was astonished a few minutes later when Don's phone rang and it turned out that Ben Hogan was, in fact, on the other end of the phone line. I couldn't hear Ben Hogan's words of the ensuing conversation, but I did hear Don's remarks. It went like this:

> Hello, Ben, this is Don…
> Yea, Ben, Don Oliver…
> Don Oliver, sports editor for the *Abilene Reporter-News*, Ben…
> I met you last year at the Colonial, Ben…
> Yea, Ben, good to talk to you too.

Then Don hung up the telephone and Don and the other men began discussing other ideas for the Bobby Morrow celebration.

*****

There were many different reporters, general news reporters, sports reporters, society reporters, and others. We typed our columns on manual typewriters, and each reporter had his own desk and typewriter. The deadline for all stories to appear in the morning edition was about midnight. Then we would all depart the newsroom, which was on the second floor of the building.

Another interesting telephone conversation that I recall occurred a couple of hours before the midnight deadline for the morning edition of the paper. It involved another reporter, Sam Emerson. Emerson was what we called a field reporter. His job was to cover stories that occurred in the surrounding rural counties and small towns. Just before deadline for the morning edition of the paper, someone called to our attention that a fatal car collision had just occurred near one of the small area towns and one fatality was the wife of the county sheriff. This, of course, would be a front-page story for the morning edition of the paper. However, since it had happened only a couple of hours before deadline, it seemed to most of us that it would be impossible to call the sheriff and inquire about the crash. To our surprise, Sam said, "I will get that story," and picked up the phone. He spoke to the receptionist downstairs and requested she call the county sheriff. We all listened to the conversation that followed.

"Sheriff this is Sam Emerson, reporter from the *Abilene Reporter-News*. I heard your wife just got killed in a car wreck."

Then we all listened in horrified silence while Emerson continued to interrogate the sheriff about all the details of the collision. *When did the accident happen? Where did it happened? How did the accident happen? Any other vehicles involved?*

To our amazement, the sheriff seemed to be answering all the reporter's questions. But the reporter's last question caused all of us to shudder.

"Well, sheriff, did she bleed a lot?"

*****

One night after the midnight deadline, everyone left, except one of the reporters. He was still composing his column for the next day. As he sat at his desk concentrating on his column, about one o'clock in the morning a fellow he had never seen before came into the newsroom. Expecting the newsroom to be empty, the stranger was obviously surprised to find someone still working. But then he quickly recovered and came up with this explanation.

"Gee whiz," he exclaimed, wiping his forehead, "I'm running late tonight. They hired me to clean all these typewriters before the morning shift arrives." Then looking at the columnist pecking away he said, "You know, I've got to get all of these typewriters, take them down to my truck, haul them to my workshop, clean all of them, change the ribbons, and return them before the morning shift arrives for work. I'm already way behind." Then he looked over at the reporter and asked, "Would you please help me load all of these typewriters into my truck so I can finish the job by the time the morning shift arrives?" The sportswriter agreed to help him, and thus the two began grabbing typewriters and heading downstairs to the stranger's truck, coming back and forth, and continuing until all typewriters were loaded in the truck, all except the sports editor's typewriter. The stranger told him to go ahead and continue his work and he would come back later and service his machine.

That was the last time anybody ever saw those typewriters. The next morning, when all the evening edition reporters and editors arrived for work, there was not one single typewriter left in the second-floor newsroom except for the sports reporter's typewriter. There was a mad dash around the town of Abilene when a herd of reporters began rushing around begging to borrow a typewriter to complete the evening edition. The strange typewriter repairman was never seen again.

*****

After my work as a reporter for the *Abilene Reporter-News*, I sought and succeeded in being hired as a reporter for the *Amarillo Globe-News*. Fred Post was the editor of the paper and the person who hired me. He was a man of few words and an authoritarian character that reminded me of General George Patton. I had worked at the newspaper for several months and not heard a word from Fred, when one day I received a note from him telling me to report to his office. I thought, *Oh my God, what have I done, is he going to fire me, reprimand me, or what?*

The next day, I walked up to his office in the corner of the newsroom. I knocked on his door and looked through the window. Fred was seated at his desk shuffling papers. He looked up, saw me, and motioned with his head for me to come in, which I did. I sat down in a chair across the desk from him to await my fate. Still no words had escaped from Fred's lips.

Let me interrupt my story to set the stage for what happened next. Both the Amarillo and the Lubbock daily newspapers were owned by the wealthy Whittenburg family, who also owned a large ranch in the Texas panhandle. They were known as a very pompous, politically conservative family who would put up with no politically liberal nonsense printed in their two newspapers. Shortly before Fred Post summoned me to his office that day, an *Amarillo* paper news reporter named Al Dewlen had resigned. He had done so just before a book titled *The Bone Pickers*, which he had written, was published. *The Bone Pickers* was touted as a fiction book, but it was clearly a thinly veiled spoof of the Whittenburg family. They were so enraged they attempted to round up all copies of the book and have them destroyed. But they did not succeed in destroying all the copies, and soon everyone in the area had read it and was talking about it.

Meanwhile, I was still sitting across the desk from Fred Post wondering what my fate would be. After a while Fred looked up and said to me, "Neal, from now on you're going to be responsible for writing and editing the Sunday book page." Hew, what a relief! I might add here this was to be in addition to my daily task as a reporter, for which I was to receive no additional salary.

I said, "Yes, sir." Then I waited for a while, expecting him to give specific instructions about how to write and compose the Sunday book page. Instead, he said nothing and continued to shuffle papers on his desk.

Finally, I decided this was the end of my conference with him. I got up and started to leave his office, but just as I reached the door, Fred looked up and said, "Neal, I better never see one damn word on that book page about the f____ *Bone Pickers.*"

"Yes, sir," I said again, and departed.

*****

After Hours with Rosie

All of us rookie reporters for the *Amarillo Globe-News* were assigned to putting together the morning edition of the paper and that meant that our deadline was about midnight. A few of us rookie reporters looked forward to the extraordinary entertainment that would follow after leaving the newspaper office. Most of us headed for the local bar a few blocks down the street.

The bar closed about one in the morning, but that was when the fun really began. The bartender at that time was a young lady named Rosie. Rosie had beautiful blonde hair and a voluptuous body. We congregated at the bar in time to get a good seat and order drinks. At closing time, if the only customers left in the bar were customers that Rosie knew she could trust, she would turn out the outside lights and lock the door.

She would continue to serve drinks from the bar because she knew that we would keep drinking for at least another couple of hours while she did a special performance just for us. She would disrobe completely and strut her stuff, giving a performance that any stripper would envy. She knew she could trust us with her secret, and we all looked forward to her performance. Rosie was a gorgeous young woman about thirty years old whose physical beauty was not the only thing we looked forward to. In addition to serving beer and cocktails, she delivered an after-hours performance that kept us in stitches and consisted of witty and wicked wisecracks, a ribald repartee of remarks, and her usual menu of insults aimed at each of us. None of us were insulted by any of her comments. It kept us all entertained, and as her performance continued her act seemed to be funnier and funnier and we laughed louder and louder and our tips grew more and more generous.

Them were the nights that we never forgot.

*****

About that same time, my college friend, Charles Cullen, who had been my sports editor when I was the editor of the Hardin-

Simmons newspaper, had managed to buy two small weekly newspapers in the Texas panhandle, both of which were located on Old Route 66—known as America's Main Street and now named Interstate 40. One was the *McLean News* that covered east of Amarillo, while the other was the *Vega Enterprise*, west of Amarillo. In my spare time I would go over and help Charley put out his weekly papers. In addition to my regular job responsibilities, I began writing a weekly column, appearing in both of Charley's papers, and I named it "Of Cabbages and Kings." I took that title from a stanza contained in the poem "The Carpenter and the Walrus," which is found in Lewis Carroll's book *Through the Looking-Glass*. It reads as follows:

> "The Time has come," the Walrus said,
> "To speak of many things
> Of shoes and ships and sealing wax,
> Of Cabbages and Kings,
> And why the sea is boiling hot,
> And whether pigs have wings."

One year the Panhandle Press Association awarded my column the honor of best column in a weekly newspaper. Following is the first "Of Cabbages and Kings" column published in the *McLean News* on March 5, 1959.

Of Cabbages & Kings
By Bill Neal

Starting a column is an awfully pretentious thing to do...like growing a mustache, sitting on the front pew or going around telling everybody your great-great third cousin on Aunt Ellie's side used to play pinochle with Benedict Arnold.

Right off the bat you run into problems, like, well, what kind of columnist to be? Or better yet, why bother with it at all? But these people—the columnist—are a hard headed lot and for one reason or another persist in trying to keep the public weaned off TV for a few minutes.

They are, to use a thoroughly absurd figure of speech, a queer kettle of fish.

A great many of these peculiar creatures are earthly philosophers who from time to time reach down into their mystic grab bags and pull out cures for various and sundry ills of mankind known and otherwise. A few take a fiendish delight in comically perverting old sayings.

Some write in unknown tongues and their columns are later set to music and become great rock 'n' roll classics.

Then come the crusaders, and this militant mob crusades about everything from meatless Tuesdays to not believing in Applehead Falls, N.J., wherever that is.

I also write nonsense...although there's no classification for it—in more polite circles. Me thinks it's sort of "soft sell" nonsense...in other words, what Maverick is to other westerns (you addicts of the one-eyed, blue-eyed monster in the living room), my stuff is to other columns. What most good columnists are, I ain't. There.

My truth-telling partner and frequent associate, C. E. Cullin, allows as how it has a great deal of consistency though.

Most writers, he says, occasionally have a bad column, but you (speaking to me, he was)... you defy the law of averages. How can you write all duds?

He further suggests that I title these humble graphs "Bird Seeds." It's for the birds.

Finally, I'm not one of those columnists who says "we" when I mean me. I have found in the past that by the use of this system I can reduce my typing by 50% when thus referring to my mother's youngest son. It also saves considerable advertising space, but I don't know just how much yet because I'm not very good with figures.

I see by one of the fillers in this issue that more suicides are committed on Wednesday than any other day of the week. That, to all weekly newspaper people, will come as no surprise.

"It's downright sinful—a shame and a disgrace—how much concrete it takes to fill up a hole, nowadays," said same partner the other day after we'd poured on a press foundation till the world looked unlevel and us with only a three-inch trowel. I suppose it's one of those modern wonders like where the yellow went or that pen-striped toothpaste.

CHAPTER 17

Me and Bull Marshall in South Dakota And Leonard Hahne's Two-Holer Trick

After my dad, Overton Boots Neal, sold the Medicine Mound Ranch, he bought a small ranch up in South Dakota along the Missouri River close to Mobridge.

We didn't stay up there all year. We ran steers on that ranch in the summer and sold them in the fall to the cattle feeders in the Midwest Corn Belt and then came back to Texas. In the summer of 1961, the summer before I went to law school, Dad sent me to South Dakota to take care of our steers.

I received a stern warning from Dad before he left for Texas, to make sure and check those cattle at least every other day. The southern boundary of our ranch was the northern boundary of the Sioux Indian Reservation which stretched out for miles and miles and miles southward over that rolling grass prairie country. Dad was concerned that if any of our cattle got out on the Indian Reservation, we would never see them again. His fears were well founded, for the nearest neighbor on the reservation was an Indian named "Bull" Marshall, who lived four or five miles south of our boundary line in the middle of nowhere. The thing that caused Dad particular concern about Bull was the fact that he had already been to the penitentiary once or twice for cattle theft.

After Dad went back to Texas, I went into Mobridge to get supplies and by chance I met Bull Marshall. He and I exchanged greetings over a drink or two in one of the numerous bars that lined the main street of Mobridge.

A few weeks later, I noticed that a couple of steers had gotten out through a water gap in a dry draw and had gone south, so I rode on down into the reservation. I wasn't too concerned with tracking them because the reservation was a rolling, virtually treeless grass country. The only trees were a few cottonwoods along the dry draws, so you could see almost forever. I kept thinking that over the next rise I would sight them. But, after I had ridden for four or five miles south and hadn't seen them and could no longer see the tracks in the tall grass, I began to get concerned.

About that time, I came up to Bull Marshall's one-room, tarpaper shack. I sat on top of the ridge for a little while and had myself a serious think. It occurred to me that Mr. Custer had run into a little difficulty with the Sioux down in this neck of the woods in the past. Nevertheless, I decided to tie up and talk to Bull. It must have been two or three o'clock that August afternoon, and the temperature had to be over one hundred degrees. But I mustered my courage and knocked on the door. To my surprise, Bull Marshall opened the door and the sight that I observed nearly floored me. I could never have guessed in a million years what Bull and his wife were doing. Bull was in his underwear, bare-chested, and he and his little German wife (who I mentally nicknamed the Cube) were sitting at the kitchen table drinking hot whiskey and—of all things—playing a game of Monopoly.

"Come right on in, Mr. Bill," Bull roared as he slapped me on the back.

I recall thinking his nickname was particularly apt.

He said, "By gollies, the wife and me, we just playin' a little Monopoly—come on in and play with us."

Without waiting for a reply, he swept the Monopoly board clean and started sorting out the money and symbols. I have to tell you, I was less than completely thrilled at the prospect. It had to have been 120 degrees in there. It stank to high heaven. Flies aplenty. And the hot whiskey they were drinking out of those old-timey glass café tumblers (no chaser, no mix, no water—

just straight, cheap, hot whiskey) wasn't exactly mint-julep-class refreshment. Nevertheless, my hosts extended me the unlimited hospitality of the house, such as it was. I figured I wasn't in much position to refuse.

I said, "Sure, I'd love to." With that I sat down and waited for Bull to get all of the Monopoly money, dice, and symbols gathered up and redistributed. Then Bull, the Cube, and me commenced playing Monopoly.

I knew one thing for sure—somehow, some way, I was going to lose that game. No Boardwalk or Park Place for me. Strictly Baltic and B&O Railroad, and I stayed in jail as many rolls as possible! I worked harder—over the next two hours—harder than I had ever worked before, to make sure I didn't win that game. But finally, I succeeded—and lost. Meanwhile, I managed to choke down enough of the hot whiskey to be polite, and also to partially anesthetize me to the heat, the flies, and the stench.

When we finally got through with that game, I immediately rose and told them how much I'd enjoyed it. Bull, of course, immediately insisted that I sit down and play another game, since I'd had the ill fortune of losing. I thanked him profusely but told him that I had to get on back to my place. I just remembered I had to meet a cattle buyer there.

As we went out the door, I said to Bull, "By the way, Bull, I noticed that a couple of my steers got through the south water gap a couple of days ago and came down here on the reservation somewhere. I just wondered if you happened to notice 'em the last day or two?"

Bull slapped me on the back and said, "By gollies, Mr. Bill, I just been so busy, I just hasn't had no chance to get out and look around. But I sure be checking around for you first chance I get."

I said, "Bull, you don't know how I'd appreciate that."

And with that, I departed.

A couple of days later, I checked the south pasture again, and, lo and behold, all the steers were present and accounted for.

Bill Neal riding Old Buck on the Neal's South Dakota ranch, circa 1961.

A couple of Saturdays later, when I was in Mobridge, I stopped by Bull's favorite watering hole, and sure enough, there he was. We greeted each other as long-lost friends and proceeded to sit down and enjoy some cool beverages, which were a whole lot more refreshing than that hot, cheap whiskey that I had endured when last we met.

At any rate, I never had any more problems losing cattle down out of the south pasture. I doubt Dad would have solved the problem the same way, but then there is more than one way to remove a cat's pelt.

Plus, I have a standing invitation to play Monopoly at Bull's place anytime.

*****

Leonard and the Two-Holer

I can't end my South Dakota story without adding at least a tidbit about another very colorful—and funny—character I met that summer. He was a German settler a few years older than me. His name was Leonard Hahne.

There were many settlers in that part of South Dakota whose ancestors had migrated from Germany. Typically, those German settlers were hardworking, serious-minded, straitlaced folks who worked their land from daylight until dark year-round.

Leonard Hahne was certainly of German stock. But Leonard, it can be safely stated, did not fit the typical mold. He was not addicted to hard work. And he couldn't be accused of being "straitlaced." He, instead, had a wonderful sense of humor and was the inventor of numerous practical jokes. Very imaginative practical jokes. Take, for instance, one he played during the summer that I was in South Dakota.

Leonard and his family lived on a small farm located only a few miles from our ranch. Near our properties, there was a very small rural town named Trail City. It had only a few businesses, one of which was a small two-pump service station. It served only a few customers, and very few of them were nonresidents. The service station did not have an indoor toilet. It provided its customers only an outhouse, which was available to both male and female customers. It was also what rural folks referred to as only a two-holer.

That fact gave Leonard a comic inspiration. He bought a microphone and a speaker device. He then hooked up the speaker under the surface of that two-holer and ran a wire to the bench located on the front porch of the service station, where he liked to sit and watch the customers when they stopped for gas.

As I pointed out, there was very little traffic to the service station and very few of them were strangers. And of those patrons only a small portion were women. While the station owner filled up their gas tanks, a few would take the occasion to use that two-holer. But Leonard was a very patient fellow. And Leonard's carefree schedule didn't require daily work on the farm, so he had lots of free time to sit on the front porch of the gas station and wait for a victim to come along.

Finally, a victim arrived—a nonresident lady who requested the owner to "fill 'er up." While the owner was "fillin' her car up," the lady took a bathroom break. She walked out to that two-holer and closed the door. Leonard waited patiently for a few minutes to give her sufficient time to get settled down and start doing her business. Then Leonard spoke into the microphone. And his voice came through loud and clear just below the lady's bare bottom.

"Excuse me, lady," Leonard said, "but would you kindly move over to that other hole. We're down here cleaning out under this one."

The lady didn't wait to get properly attired. In fact, she damn near tore the door off the two-holer getting out! The discombobulated woman then discovered that she had left her purse inside the two-holer and had to request the station owner to please go out to the outhouse and retrieve it so she could pay him for the gasoline.

Leonard, who overheard the lady's request, was such a gentleman that he kindly volunteered to retrieve her purse for her.

CHAPTER 18

Destination Law School
Heading South to Austin, Texas

The summer of 1961 while on the plains of South Dakota taking care of my dad's herd of steers, I had plenty of time to think about and seriously reflect on what occupation to pursue for the rest of my life. Time to ponder that critical decision. I had solitude aplenty from my shack on those South Dakota plains. It seemed I could see forever with no sign of civilization on the horizon.

Although I really enjoyed working at the *Amarillo Globe-News* with the rest of the news reporters, I decided I did not want to spend the rest of my life as a newspaper reporter. Working as a news reporter would not allow me to accomplish my future goals. First, I wanted to be my own boss and not spend the rest of my working career taking orders from someone else. And second, I wanted to make enough money to purchase my own ranch. But where would I go from here?

As a reporter for the Amarillo paper, I had often been assigned to stories that required me to go to the Potter County courthouse in Amarillo. On one occasion I had reported on a murder trial and I became fascinated with the trial attorneys' performances. I began thinking about a legal career and considered enrolling in law school. That would be the beginning of a new adventure. No member of my family had ever pursued a career in law. I decided to return to Texas in August and enroll in school. The University of Texas in Austin, our state capital, had the largest and best law school in the state, and that was my destination.

On my way to Austin I stopped by Hardin-Simmons University in Abilene and picked up my college records. I mistakenly believed that would be all that I needed to enter the University of Texas law school.

I soon discovered that there was a lot more to enrolling into a law school than I had anticipated. When I walked into the registrar's office, one of the things the clerk asked for was my LSAT score. I asked her, "What is an LSAT?" She informed me that it was a law school admission test that must be passed before I could seek enrollment. I said, "Well, I am ready to take that exam right now," but was told that it was administered only once a year and that was in the month of October. I left her office feeling determined to somehow enter law school that September.

The next day, I returned to the registrar's office. I told her that I needed to begin law school now and I would then take the exam in October. I could not do that, she said, because it would not comply with the admission requirements for law school. I left there for a second time but was still not ready to give up. I was determined to somehow enroll in law school that semester.

The next day, I returned for a third time, and for a third time was informed that I had to take that exam and pass it before I could enroll. I told the registrant again that I just couldn't wait another year to start law school, and with a disgruntled expression she denied my request. The next day, I returned to the registrar's office for a fourth time and I proposed this: "Let me enroll into law school now and I will take that LSAT exam in October. If I don't pass, you can throw me out of law school and I won't come back." She finally agreed to accept my proposal, although the exasperated clerk told me that they had never done that before. I was made to understand that without exception I would be dismissed in October if I did not take and pass that exam. Thus, I began my law school experience.

The first day in law school, I attended orientation. The one thing that I recall most vividly was what the law professor conducting orientation said. He informed the large group of beginning law students that we should not expect to travel an easy road to graduation. He said, for example, "Look to the student seated to your right and the student seated to your left. In all probability, only one of the three of you will graduate from law school." He was not kidding.

In my freshman year, when October arrived, I did take that exam and passed.

Law school was not easy, but I was determined that whatever it took I was going to graduate. And three years later, I did graduate.

However, there were a few amusing incidents that I enjoyed along the way. Each spring the law school had a "Fun Day." There were no classes that day, and all students and faculty members were encouraged to do an entertaining performance: a skit, a song, a poem, or some other comedic act. My favorite was the time Professor Corwin Johnson composed a poem titled, "Texas' Uncommon Laws," which he sang to the tune of "The Yellow Rose of Texas." Its theme was how wild and lawless the Texas frontier had been. It went like this:

A loyal son of Texas
Went out upon a spree,
Committed six murders,
Some rape, and burglaree.
They swung him from the gallows,
A proper end, of course;
But the reason that they hung him was
That bastard stole a horse!

*****

At the end of my freshman year, I had scored well in all my classes, and one of the law professors, Leon Lebowitz, asked me to be his quizmaster during the next school year. Quizmasters were charged with performing numerous tasks for their professors that allowed them to focus on their teaching duties: tasks like checking attendance in classes, and grading class exams that included true/false and multiple-choice questions. We did not grade test answers that required students to write an essay. Also we gathered requested law books from the library, and other mundane jobs.

During my senior year, one of the most sensational and tragic events in our nation's history occurred and it disrupted our law studies. On the morning of November 22, 1963, President John F. Kennedy was scheduled to speak in Dallas. Later that afternoon he and his wife, Jacqueline, were also going to appear in Austin. But he never arrived. In anticipation of his arrival and hearing him speak that afternoon, a couple of my law school friends and I began walking toward downtown Austin. Suddenly some fellow ran out of his home and yelled, "Somebody just shot and killed President Kennedy up in Dallas." In stunned silence we all three turned around and headed back to the school.

*****

Each year, the law school named several of the top students in the senior class to write and publish an annual edition of the University of Texas *Law Review*, and I was one of the chosen students as well as being named the comment editor that year. We were each assigned topics to research, with the supervision of a law professor, and compose an article for the booklet. It was invaluable training for future lawyers in researching and composing appellate briefs.

William O. "Bill Neal" graduated number one in the University of Texas School of Law and was named grand chancellor in 1964.

Each year the top six graduates of law school were honored as chancellors of the graduating class. I was the valedictorian of the 1964 class and was named grand chancellor. That summer, after taking and passing the Texas bar exam, I was finally an officially licensed lawyer. Later that summer, I received another honor. I was hired as a briefing attorney for one of the nine justices of the Texas Supreme Court. Justice Ruel C. Walker hired me to serve as his briefing attorney for one year. When the next session of the court began in the fall of that year at the Supreme Court building in Austin, I reported to Judge Walker and began a year of exciting and illuminating legal experience.

When a state court trial is held, the losing attorney will sometimes submit a written appeal to the Texas Supreme Court. If the court accepts the legal appeal, then a public hearing is held. Each briefing attorney present reads the appellate briefs and listens closely to the oral arguments. Sometime within the next few weeks, the justices hold a private meeting and exchange views regarding the proper disposition of the appeal. Although the briefing attorneys are not allowed to express views, we are permitted to sit in and hear the judges debate. At the end of the debate, one of the judges is selected to write a summary of the court's opinion and verdict, and if there is a split decision between the judges, then one or more of the dissenting judges will write a dissenting opinion, which also will be published.

At that point the judge who is to write the court's opinion will assign his or her briefing attorney the task of researching and writing the judge's proposed opinion, and that is when the briefing attorneys go to work reading all the briefs and heading for the court's law library and writing a proposed opinion. I recall one case where there was a heated exchange between two judges about the court's decision. One of the judges was Chief Justice Robert Calvert. Judge Calvert and another of the judges had such a heated argument they were yelling at each other about the court's proposed decision, and I thought they might end up in a fistfight. But before that happened the court took a break for lunch.

Afterward, as we were all strolling to a nearby café, I noticed Judge Calvert and the judge with whom he had just heatedly debated began having a very cordial conversation. Not a word was exchanged between them regarding the legal debate. I was trailing along listening and afterward remarked to Judge Calvert how surprised I was to see how friendly the two men had become after almost coming to blows shortly before in the courtroom debate.

Judge Calvert, whom I had come to admire greatly, smiled and made this comment, a comment I have frequently recalled: "Well, Bill, you know, just because somebody has a very different opinion on an issue, it doesn't mean that he is a bad person or necessarily wrong in his opinion of the matter. In fact, it may not necessarily mean that his opinion is all wrong and yours is all right. It could mean that neither one of you is exactly right. There could be a third view that is closer to the correct view." As a briefing attorney that year, I learned a lot, and not only about Texas law.

Although Judge Calvert was a Democrat and had won his seat on the Texas Supreme Court as its chief justice, he once grinned and commented to me that he was kind of a "foot-dragging liberal." He was raised as an orphan, had worked his way through law school, had been elected to the Texas House of Representatives, and next was elected as Speaker of the House, and later as chief justice of the Texas Supreme Court.

A couple of times during that year, Judge Calvert invited all of the briefing attorneys to his home on a Saturday night to a very enjoyable evening.

Meanwhile, during that year, when it came Judge Ruel Walker's time to write an opinion for the court, he had me research and write a proposed opinion for him. In compliance, I went to the supreme court's library, spent considerable time researching the issues, and then composed a draft of an opinion to present to Judge Walker. I was proud of my effort. I had done painstaking research on the issues, and since I had been a newspaper reporter, I felt I had submitted a well-written proposed opinion. Then Judge Walker took it and rewrote it as the Supreme Court's official opinion. After I read his official opinion, I realized I still had a long way to go in my legal career.

*****

After earning the honor of being named grand chancellor of my law school class and then serving as a briefing attorney for the Texas Supreme Court, I was offered jobs with very impressive salaries to join large law firms in Houston, Dallas, and Austin. Tall-building law firms, I called them. Instead, I chose to return to my small West Texas hometown of Quanah. I took a position working for a local attorney, Lark Bell, at a very reduced salary.

However, I was still determined to become my own boss and eventually make enough money to buy my own ranch. In the fall of 1967, I decided to run for district attorney of a three-county district, the Forty-sixth Judicial District. I ran against the incumbent district attorney and one other local attorney and was elected for a four-year term beginning January 1, 1968. At the end of that term, I ran for a second term and won. My office was in Vernon, in Wilbarger County. I had finally become my own boss. Now, it only remained to achieve my other goal. I would also accomplish buying my own ranch, but it would take a while.

CHAPTER 19

Now You Are Told The Time I Prosecuted a Victimless Crime

I want to tell you a true story. I swear it's all true. Every word. I've got a pretty good imagination, but I'm here to testify that I couldn't have made this one up. Even if I'd quaffed down a few too many.

It's all about the time when I was a young lawyer and serving my first term as the district attorney of a rural three-county district up in northwest Texas just below the corner of the Texas panhandle. As I recall, it happened about 1970 or 1971.

Well, let's get to the point: I was called upon to prosecute what I referred to as a "victimless crime." Three parties were involved in this "affair," so to speak, and not a one was complaining. Nobody was murdered, injured, endangered, threatened by anybody, or had lost any property. And nobody else was complaining either. No victim as far as I could see. And no villain either. Or…were there three villains?

The only folks raising a ruckus about the whole episode were the good folks of Vernon, county seat of Wilbarger County, who had elected me district attorney.

Hold on, I'll get back to that in a minute.

First, let me introduce the three characters in this—I'm searching for a word here—"drama," "farce," "comedy," "an unpleasant intrusion on the privacy of three semi-innocent lives," or…If I were just as good a storyteller as Mark Twain, I might be able to come up with better adjectives and thus do justice to this…ah, "incident." Anyhow,

I'll flounder around and do the best I can to get on with it. As I mentioned, there were three parties involved in this victimless crime: Two of the parties were a married couple in their fifties—Arthur and Ima Bell Werline—who lived on the outskirts of the town of Vernon, the poor section of town. Some folks called them "poor white trash." They were poor folks and they were white, all right, but "trashy"? I think that's a bit too harsh. Arthur and Ima Bell lived in a rundown shack with a large barn behind it. Neither Arthur nor Ima Bell had any prior criminal record. The third party was a male. I don't think anybody ever told me his name, but he was about ten years old and Arthur and Ima Bell kept him in their barn. That's because he was a Shetland stud pony. Very gentle and very well mannered.

Now, let me introduce the other participants in this drama: myself, a native son from those parts who hadn't been out of law school but maybe five or six years. Just elected as district attorney in the last election. I'd run against the incumbent and won. The incumbent's secretary was named Ola Mae McCaleb and she was in her fifties and had been his secretary for a number of years. I liked Ola Mae and didn't want to throw her out of a job, so I talked her into staying on as my secretary. We got along well even though we were cut from very different cloth: Ola Mae was a very dedicated Christian—a Baptist—and I was more, well, relaxed and casual, even fun-loving, some said. Although Ola Mae was married but with no children, she sometimes gave the impression of being a prim and proper "old maid."

Then there was my investigator, Lewis Yoakum. I didn't have any assistant district attorney under me—I had to take on all the felony criminal cases in the district myself while the county attorney in each of my three counties handled all the misdemeanor crimes. Anyway, Lewis was even more fun-loving and relaxed than I was, and his sense of humor registered about nine and a half on the Richter scale. Lewis was not a lawyer, and when I hired him as my investigator, he didn't have a lick of experience in investigating or in courtroom justice. But Lewis never met a stranger. He was well liked in that area, and he knew most of the folks. He had been a local football hero in high school and afterward had been hired as sports editor of the local newspaper. With his background and personality, I figured he could find out just about everything on anybody in that rural district and about everything that was going on, and that, after all, was what I needed from an investigator. Plus, when it came to selecting folks for a jury, who better to advise me on how each prospective juror might lean in any kind of case?

So, there we were, up in our little cubbyhole office on the third floor of the Wilbarger County courthouse the day the Werline case broke. Ola Mae was out front that day in her office serving as my secretary, receptionist, and telephone answerer, while Lewis and I worked in our smaller offices behind hers. Right here I need to mention this: When the Werline case broke, Ola Mae mentioned to Lewis and me that she knew the Werlines. How? Well, she said that several months previously when the local Baptist Church had held a revival, she had gone from house to house just before that revival knocking on doors and inviting folks to attend. It was during that excursion that she met and visited with Arthur and Ima Bell. I'm sure Ola Mae lived to regret giving Lewis and me that tidbit of information about her relationship with the Werlines. Afterward, when just the three of us were in our office and nobody else was listening, Lewis and I—when talking between ourselves, but within Ola Mae's hearing—would refer to the Werlines as "Ola Mae's friends."

*****

Now, let me tell you about the first time I heard about the alleged crime that the Werlines had committed. Nobody in the local law enforcement community—not any of the cops—had ever mentioned the Werlines to me or consulted with me about filing any criminal charges against them. (I'd never heard about the Werlines before that day.) How did the Werlines' alleged crime come to the attention of a local crime-stopper?

Apparently, Ima Bell, not realizing that there was anything illegal, immoral, or even unusual about the threesome's affair, had casually mentioned something about it to a neighbor lady. The shocked neighbor lady—when she recovered her senses—made a beeline dash to the local sheriff's office and spilled the beans, so to speak. The sheriff immediately dispatched a deputy to investigate.

The next time the law-abiding neighbor lady observed Arthur and Ima Bell enter their barn, she got on the phone and alerted the sheriff. A deputy raced out to the Werline homestead and peeked through a crack in the old barn and…sure 'nuff, the love triangle participants were caught in the act. Other local cops were summoned, and without bothering to notify the county attorney or me, the whole posse raced out to the Werlines' barn and without warrant handcuffed Arthur and Ima Bell. The third party was left in the barn. Arthur and Ima Bell in tow, they raced back to the courthouse and up to the third floor they came. And what a clamor and racket they were making.

Ola Mae, Lewis, and I had been calmly sitting in our nest occupied with routine paperwork when the dam broke and the sheriff and several deputies—all trying to talk at the same time—came barreling into the office and began babbling away, trying to inform us of the Werlines' horrific crime. Meanwhile, Arthur and Ima Bell were sitting quietly on a bench outside my office—unsupervised and unguarded. I asked the excited posse if they'd taken any statements from the accused. Said they hadn't. "Good," I said. "I'll take it from here." Finally, I shooed them out of my office, and they retreated.

While all this was going on, news of this sensational crime had spread like wildfire throughout the Vernon community. I began to get phone calls: "What's all this scandalous talk going around about a naked woman and a…and a….?"

I filled in the gap: "Horse?"

"Yep," the caller replied.

Then I said, "We got it straight from the horse's mouth."

After I got rid of all the cops, I brought Ima Bell into my office and parked Arthur in Yoakum's office. Read her rights to her. Told her she could have a lawyer if she wanted one. She looked at me with a puzzled look and shook her head. Then I asked what had happened.

"Well, they all come a-runnin' into our barn and grabbed me and Arthur and hauled us down here."

"Did they leave your horse there?"

"Yep."

I have to make a confession at this point. I was really more curious about the mechanics of her romp with her four-legged boyfriend than I was with possible criminal violations. Was she ashamed? Think she'd done something wrong? How long had this been going on? What did Arthur think about it? Was he just an observer or was he a participant? To all these questions, Ima Bell didn't balk, bat an eye, or hesitate to answer.

"Oh, yes," she assured me, Arthur set up the stage, put the bridle on her boyfriend, and then led the pony to the position so he could mount her, adding that Arthur then took Polaroid pictures of the amorous pair in action. To all these explanations Ima Bell was about as matter-of-fact as if she had been telling me how she cooked up a mess of collard greens. I nodded understandingly and kept listening.

When she paused, I casually asked her if she and her husband, Arthur, ever…you know …uh…did it together?

"Oh, yes," she replied, "but you know ole' Arthur, he's got so old he can't hardly do it no more…you know…more than once a day."

"Oh," I said, sympathetically nodding my head while biting my tongue and struggling to freeze my face.

Back to the mechanics? Arthur, she explained, got one of those rectangular bales of hay, the ones about three or four feet long, two feet wide, and about two and a half or three feet high, and he put a blanket over it. Ima Bell then lay down on it on her tummy, presenting herself to her boyfriend in a "doggie-style" position. Arthur then led the boyfriend to the right place and assisted them in the coupling. Then he got his camera out.

At that point our conversation had progressed so calmly and pleasantly that Ima Bell began asking me questions. She questioned me about my family: Did I live in Vernon? Was I married? Have any kids? What about my parents? And so on. In return, I asked about her family: any children? Turned out they had two kids who were grown and had moved out of the home. She and Arthur were from Oklahoma. Had recently moved to Vernon, and Arthur had gotten part-time work on farms. And so on. (The town of Vernon, by the way, is only about fifteen miles south of the Red River, the south boundary of Oklahoma.)

Then I casually brought the conversation back to the barn. To their "affair."

And Ima Bell continued to explain. Once she nearly caused me to lose composure. Out of the blue she said: "You know, Arthur was kinda worried that that pony might knock me up. But I don't think so. Do you?" Trying desperately not to convulse and fall backward out of my chair, I gripped my desk and leaned forward and dropped my head as if to give the matter serious consideration. Meantime, a vision flashed in my mind: What would a half horse, half Ima Bell look like? And which half would be Ima Bell—top or bottom half? Bottom half, I bet! Finally, I took a deep breath and looked up—assured Ima Bell that I really didn't think she had anything to worry about.

There was another legal question I needed to clear up if indeed all this came down to a sodomy trial. I needed to know if the horse's penis had actually penetrated her vagina. Under Texas law there had to be some penetration, but the appellate court had interpreted that to mean that *any* penetration, "however slight," was sufficient to make the case. So bringing the subject up as casually and as matter-of-factly as I could, I asked the question something like this: "You know, Ima Bell, I was just, you know, kinda...well, wondering if he...I mean...uh, you know did...well, I mean, did he really get his...uh, his thing into your thing, you know...back there?"

Ima Bell didn't blink or hesitate. "Oh, yes," she said, then holding her left arm out toward me, she took the index finger on her right hand and pointed to a place on her left arm about two or three inches below her elbow. "About that far," she explained.

"Oh," I said. "Ah...okay."

Gripping my chair's arms, biting my tongue, and face-freezing again.

And while I was attempting to regain my mental equilibrium from that revelation, another thought whizzed through my brain: If a grand jury indicted Ima Bell and Arthur for sodomy, wouldn't they be obliged to also indict Ima Bell's four-legged boyfriend? Surely not!

Oh, and there's one more thing I almost forgot to mention: Arthur's Polaroid pictures. Before the cops left the Werlines' barn, they gathered up a few of Arthur's pictures. I was anxious to view them. Pornographic, no doubt, but also very instructive—revealing the mechanics of the setup. But they were neither pornographic nor instructive. I don't know whether Arthur was so nervous or so excited or just such a terrible photographer, but the pictures were way off target, out of focus, and blurry. Blurry maybe, but one thing was absolutely clear: Arthur would never, ever get a shot at shooting pictures for the centerfold of the next *Playboy* magazine.

Truthfully, I can't now recall exactly how Ima Bell's next jaw-dropping revelation came about, but in the interim I'd learned that while she and Arthur were still living in Oklahoma and before they moved to Texas, they had somehow become friends with other folks—both men and women—who also enjoyed similar sexual sports with animals. So, when I'd made some remark to Ima Bell to the effect that having a sexual experience with a pony was the first I'd ever heard about such goings-on, she corrected me, informed me that some of the men and women they had known over in Oklahoma had coupled with horses, and cows, and goats, and…even chickens! I shook my head at this incredulous information and remarked: "Oh, I had no idea!"

To which Ima Bell calmly replied: "Well, now you are told."

I never forgot that line. A real classic.

Later, I shared Ima Bell's classic remark with some of my family and friends. And still to this day, when one of us makes an observation that draws a response like "I didn't know that," then the revealer borrows Ima Bell's response and retorts: "Well, now you are told!"

After I had completed my interview with Ima Bell and reduced the principal parts to writing, Ola Mae, shaking her head in disbelief, struggled mightily to type it all up. When she finished, Ima Bell glanced at it, nodded, and signed her name without comment.

Then I interviewed Arthur. While he was not nearly as chatty or as colorful as Ima Bell, he also nodded—didn't challenge any of the basic points in Ima Bell's statement. Only one slight difference.

Arthur "allowed as how" the "affair" was all Ima Bell's idea. Ima Bell had said, not quite as convincingly, that it was all Arthur's idea.

Either way, neither had balked at taking pen in hand and signing off on the story.

Afterward, Lewis and I stayed amused for days exchanging Ima Bell's classic punch lines, and, when within Ola Mae's hearing, we would refer to Arthur and Ima Bell as "Ola Mae's friends." Perhaps, in retrospect, we were acting like a couple of smart-aleck kids with a new toy.

One day, when nobody was in the office except the three of us, and Lewis was in my office and I knew Ola Mae could hear us, I winked at Lewis and said, "You know, Lewis, I been thinking, if the Werline case comes down to a jury trial, you'll be sitting as usual with me at the prosecutor's table helping me with the papers and stepping out to summon the next witness, and you know, we'll have to have somebody lead that Shetland pony into the courtroom, since I'll have to introduce him into evidence as State's Exhibit number one."

That was a big fib; it wasn't necessary to introduce the horse into evidence, and Lewis was aware of that—but another wink at Lewis and I continued. "Tell you what we'll do, I'll get some deputy to haul the stud horse up to the courthouse and put a halter on him. Then put him in the elevator [I doubted he really would fit into the elevator, but I continued] and bring him up to the third floor, and then I'll get Ola Mae to lead him into the courtroom so the jury can see him when I introduce him into evidence." Wink, wink. We could hear Ola Mae gasp.

Nevertheless, even if I didn't view the Werline matter as a serious criminal offense—one that would endanger the health, safety, or welfare of the community—still, after all the hubbub that the Werline triangle had touched off and the repeated phone calls I received from local folks—I figured I had better at least protect myself come next election by presenting the matter to a grand jury. Which is what I did. I reckoned that the grand jurors would probably not view the matter as a serious threat to us good, law-abiding citizens and would move on to more serious prison-deserving acts of real criminals.

I reckoned wrong. Much to my surprise, when I laid out the case to the grand jurors, those folks took it very seriously and indicted both Arthur and Ima Bell. But not Ima Bell's boyfriend.

I still suspect that at least some of the grand jurors might have felt that the Werlines didn't deserve to be dragged through a criminal trial and sentenced to prison, but perhaps were afraid to vote against an indictment, fearing that word might be whispered around town that they approved of such appalling misbehavior.

But when I got back to my office and considered the matter, I realized that I was in a terrible predicament. I couldn't prosecute that case before a jury and keep a straight face. And, if I gave a half-hearted effort trying the case and the jury found them not guilty? Wow! That wouldn't do. After all the public uproar the Werline case had touched off, I couldn't move to dismiss the case. In view of the grand jurors' reaction, I doubted I could survive the next district attorney election if I did. Besides all that, I seriously doubted that if I let the Werlines off easy, it would encourage any other citizens to buy a Shetland stud horse and take up the Werlines' sport. Well, I thought, maybe I could recuse myself and bring in an outside prosecutor. But what if he got a conviction and it triggered a similar reaction as the grand jurors had displayed and demanded a lengthy prison sentence? Maybe Arthur and Ima Bell were just "poor white trash," but did that mean they ought to be sent to prison for years, plus taking up space in a Texas penitentiary when there were plenty of real thugs out there who needed to be removed from preying on the public?

So, what to do?

I had Arthur and Ima Bell brought up to my office for a private conference. And I again asked if they wanted a lawyer. Told them they had a right to have one appointed by the judge if they couldn't pay for one. Both said they didn't want one, and I could sense that those poor country hicks were trusting me to "do the right thing." Finally, I said this: "If you want to get this thing behind us, what about doing this: I'll find a day real soon when the judge is in town and isn't holding court, and I'll have him bring you over and you all tell him you don't need a lawyer but are ready to plead guilty. Then

I'll recommend a two-year prison sentence as your punishment, but you won't have to go to jail. See, I'll recommend the judge put both of you on probation for two years. No jail time, no fine, no probation fees." (You could do that back in 1970, at least in our district.) And then, I reassured the Werlines that if they wanted to go back to Oklahoma it would be okay with me, and I wouldn't hold it against them. In fact, I told them that it would probably be a real good idea if they did go back to Oklahoma, considering how the local folks seemed to be very upset with them. They agreed, and so it played out that way, and I got the criminal case resolved without a trial. And I got the Werlines out of town—and out of state, for that matter.

They did go back to Oklahoma, and I reckoned that I'd gotten shed of that case. And of the Werlines. All without going to trial. Had heard the last of them.

But I was wrong. I hadn't heard the last of the Werlines.

Sometime later, I think it was about a year or so, but it was while they were still on probation, I got a call from an Oklahoma prosecutor. He informed me that they had the Werlines in their jail. Asked me if we didn't still have them on probation "for messing around with a horse?" I hated to admit it, but I didn't want to lie, so I told him that we did. Then he informed me that they had been caught "doing the same damned thing" over there. Said that they had admitted it, that they were in jail, that they had confessed and signed off on written confessions, and that they had also waived extradition back to Texas. Said that all I needed to do was just file a motion to revoke their probation, get a warrant for their arrest, and send a deputy over to pick them up.

Then he asked when I could send a deputy over there. I told him that while I sympathized with him, I wasn't going to send a deputy over there to retrieve the Werlines.

"What?" he exclaimed.

"Yep," I said.

Then he growled, "What the hell kind of district attorney are you anyway?"

Then I said, "I'm the kind of district attorney that doesn't want any more to do with the Werlines. You got 'em, you keep 'em. Bye now."

And then I hung up.

*****

I practiced law for forty years, doing many criminal law cases, sometimes as a prosecutor, sometimes as a defense attorney, but I never had any criminal case anything like the Werline case. And for about half that time, and until she retired, Ola Mae was my faithful secretary. She never missed a day showing up for work.

Except that day when the Werlines appeared in court to plead guilty. I think Ola Mae really believed (or hoped!) that I was kidding about making her lead that stud horse into the courtroom.

But she wasn't taking any chances!

*****

Arthur Milton Werline
1924–1993

Ima Bell Farrow Werline
1929–1996

Arthur and Ima Bell are buried in the Belleville-Bourland
Cemetery, Courtney, Love County, Oklahoma

CHAPTER 20

The Looser the Fit, the Tighter the Noose Divorce Her on *What* Ground!

I'm going to call him "Jason Blake." That's not his real name, but even though he died several years ago, I don't want to besmirch his name or embarrass his descendants. And for the same reason, I'll call his wife "Mildred." And I'll refer to the county where it all happened as "NWTX" County.

One day, back in the 1970s, I was sitting in my private law office shuffling papers when Jason came bustin' through my office door (didn't bother to knock or say "howdy" to my secretary) and blurted: "Get me a divorce!"

I had never represented Jason before and was not a close friend, although I did know him. Jason was in his late fifties or early sixties and was a prosperous farmer who lived in a rural community tucked just under the southeast corner of the Texas panhandle. Jason lived in a big home (just shy of what you'd call a mansion) that was located on his large farm. Had a couple of big barns, some livestock, tractors, plows, and other farming equipment, plus three big combines (for harvesting wheat), trucks, pickups, and a couple of new cars parked in his garage. For a number of years Jason had operated a very successful custom wheat-harvesting business with those three combines and several trucks to haul the harvested wheat to area elevators. Jason began each year in the early summer harvesting wheat for various farmers in North Texas and then following the harvest as the wheat ripened in fields to the north. Customarily, he followed the harvest and was gone from his Texas home for about three months.

Jason was married and had been for some thirty-five or forty years. I've forgotten exactly how many, but it had been quite a spell, and insofar as I knew it had been a successful marriage. Nevertheless, here he came storming in my office that day, demanding a divorce. Immediately! As if all I had to do was to run over to the courthouse, collar the judge, and order him to sign a divorce judgment.

I tried to calm him down. But nothing doing. He went on rantin', ravin', and cussin'—called his wife, alternately, a "bitch," a "whore," a "slut," all the while adding quite an impressive vocabulary of profane adjectives. Finally, when he ran out of steam for a few breaths, I asked Jason if Mildred had run off with another man while he was gone on his wheat-harvesting tour.

"Nope."

"Is she still living at home with you?"

"Yep."

Then he cranked up and lit into another barrage of such language as a body would never hear inside church doors.

"Well, Jason," I said, "did you catch her in the act?"

"Nope."

I kept thinking he was going to tell me how he knew that Mildred was fooling around on him. But no. He launched into another profane rant.

"Well, Jason," I said, "did somebody tell you about Mildred's affair?"

"Nope."

Then, red in the face and sprinkling spit on his overalls, he started into another tirade.

This time when he ran down, I jumped in and demanded: "Well, Jason, if Mildred is still living with you, and she didn't admit to an affair, and you didn't catch her in the act, and nobody told you about it, then how in the hell do you know she's having an affair with another man?"

This time Jason didn't fire back immediately with another obscene volley. Instead he got quiet. Didn't utter a word. Sorta tucked his head for a bit, hooked his thumbs in the galluses of his overalls, and then, in a much lower voice—and speaking very slowly—muttered: "Well, Bill, you know, I reckon I got the littlest dick in NWTX County, and when I left on the harvest it fit, but when I came back, it didn't."

"Oh," I said, "...uh...well...uh...I see."

After a long silence, I steered the conversation in another direction. "Jason," I said, "before I file a divorce suit for you, we need to talk about your property. When a divorce is granted, the court will divide your property, and so I will need a list of all your property, the land, the home, the combines, the trucks, cars, pickups, tractors, plows, livestock, bank accounts, and so on. Also, whatever debts you have. Then we have to list what items of property are community property owned by you and Mildred, and what items of property are yours separately." Then I explained to Jason that he would have to determine the fair market value of all his property and so forth and so on.

The property discussion went on for about two and a half hours. Jason listened, nodded occasionally, and seemed to take it all in. I could tell it set him back on his heels. Obviously, he hadn't thought about property divisions and values in his outrage against that sorry, no-good, cheatin' hussy. It was obvious that when Jason stormed into the office he must have figured that when the judge heard about Mildred's terrible misconduct and unforgivable sins he would "throw the book at her," grant the divorce, award Jason all the property, and then focus on Mildred: deliver a sermon—a mere lecture wouldn't do; it would take one of those old-timey, red-hot pulpit-poundin', Bible-thumpin' rants to really humiliate and humble her.

Finally, I dismissed Jason. Told him to go home and start work on his property inventory and estimate the market values. Jason got up quietly and departed.

After he left, I called my secretary and told her to hold the calls for a spell. Then I sat back, let my brain-fog clear, and had myself a big think. And it wasn't about Jason's property inventory and appraisement. It was about Jason's determination to divorce and humiliate his wife. And his ground for divorce—and his only ground for divorce: adultery. But how the hell could I prove to a judge and jury that Mildred had committed adultery?

I'd done pretty well in law school, and I'd tried some nasty, mud-slinging divorce cases—especially child custody cases—but nothing like Jason's case. Would it be a heart-breaking tearjerker? A bawdy comedy? Or both?

Either way, since Jason would be the plaintiff, I'd have the burden of proving that Mildred had committed adultery while Jason was off harvesting wheat. I'd have to call Jason as my first witness. He'd have to lay the foundation: "I reckon I've got the littlest dick in NWTX County."

No, Jason couldn't afford to phrase it that way. Maybe I could coach him to tone it down a bit, something like: "Well, you know, I reckon I'm only blessed with a very small piece of equipment down there," meanwhile pointing below the waist.

But then what? Somehow, we'd then have to shift focus to Mildred's endowment below her waist—that snug fit she had before Jason left for a three-month wheat harvest, but a much looser fit after his return.

Even though I like to think I'm a pretty good cross-examiner of adverse witnesses, I couldn't, in my wildest imagination, believe I could ever browbeat Jason's wife into admitting that the fit was a lot looser when Jason returned. Or that she was guilty of adultery while he was gone. Even if the court ordered both parties to submit to a physical examination, and even if the doctor confirmed Jason's contention that the fit was indeed loose down there, there's no way he could verify Jason's assertion that the fit had been snug before he left on harvest.

Plus, I could just imagine the parade of character witnesses Jason's wife would summon—particularly members of her church and her social club, all of whom would no doubt swear to the judge and jury that Mildred was a wonderful high-class lady and a dedicated Christian.

Anyway, the more I thought about it, the more ridiculous—and impossible—it seemed. I don't believe even Clarence Darrow could have found a crack (excuse the pun) in Mildred's denial of any adulterous misconduct.

I shook my head. I picked up the phone and told my secretary to go ahead and put through any calls. Maybe…I thought… just maybe Jason would realize how much money and property a divorce would cost him. And just maybe that would cause him to calm down. And stare reality in the face.

*****

I didn't see Jason anymore for six weeks or so, until one day I met him walking down the sidewalk near my office. "Jason," I said, "have you finished the inventory and appraisement of your property yet?"

"Nah," he shrugged, and kept on walking down the street. And that's the last I ever heard from Jason about divorcing that soiled dove-wife of his. I reckoned that Jason recalled all those many hot summer days that he'd spent over the years sweatin' and steamin' in dust-chokin' wheat fields in order to accumulate his fortune.

And after giving the matter a more calm, mature, and sober consideration, Jason must have concluded that a slightly enlarged entranceway wasn't quite a matter of such cosmic magnitude as he'd originally concluded.

CHAPTER 21

Odor in the Car And Order in the Courtroom

One Sunday afternoon, I went to my law office in Vernon and worked to get ready for a jury trial that was scheduled to begin the next morning in the district court in Quanah. It was almost sundown when I left the office. I got into my Volkswagen and started down the road heading for my ranch home. It was about dusk as I was traveling along that country road when I ran over a raccoon crossing the road. I stopped, backed up, and examined the dead raccoon. He was a really large one and his pelt would make a nice decoration on the wall at my ranch home. I grabbed him, opened the trunk at the front of the Volkswagen, and slung that raccoon in and closed the lid. Then I drove on home.

The next morning, I was in the bathroom shaving when I remembered that raccoon was still in my Volkswagen trunk. I went outside, in only my underwear and shoes, opened the lid of the trunk, and got one of the most unexpected surprises of my life. That coon was not dead! And he was mad as hell. He reared up on his hind legs and glared at me for a long spell. Then he gave out a snarling low growl. He had awakened several hours earlier and finding himself in a dark confining space had scrambled for an escape. It was obvious that he had tried to escape his jail cell for hours because he had deposited a gooey liquid and solid stinking excrement all over the place! When he saw me he glared at me with murderous intent in his eyes. I picked up a dead tree limb and whacked him and pulled him out of the trunk. This time I made sure that he was dead.

With the raccoon adequately dispatched, I looked at the stinking mess he had deposited in the trunk of my car. No way could I drive to court in that car stinking like an outdoor john. I had to grab a water hose and wash out that mess. And that was not easy! Or quick. The clock was running, and by the time I finished, I knew the judge and a courtroom of prospective jurors would be assembling in the Hardeman County district courtroom fifteen miles down the road. I jumped into the shower and grabbed a suit and dashed for my car. I knew that by the time I arrived at the courthouse everyone would already be assembled.

When I parked and jumped out of my car and started running across the courthouse lawn, I saw a prospective juror also quickly heading across the lawn. She was late for jury duty. I recognized her. Her name was Rhonda Brown, a good friend of mine and the wife of Bob Brown, an area rancher. I said hi and kept jogging across the lawn.

Rhonda then raced up to me and said, "Bill, I know something you don't know."

I was in no mood to stop and visit. So I just grunted, "Oh. What?" What Rhonda said next did stop me midstride.

"Your pants are not zipped up."

I zipped up my pants and finally entered the courtroom. The room was filled with folks there for possible jury duty, and the judge—Judge Rex Sullivan—was already on the bench asking prospective jurors if anyone had some unexpected or personal emergency in their life that would justify being excused from serving as a juror. One man held up his hand. He was a Mexican migrant who lived in the county and worked as a farm laborer. Judge Sullivan asked him to explain his reason for asking to be excused from jury duty. He replied. "Well, Mr. Judge, my wife, she is expecting to become pregnant tomorrow." There was a silent pause. Suddenly giggles started and the whole crowd erupted with laughter. Then another prospective juror raised his hand. Judge Sullivan quieted the crowd and called the courtroom to order. The second juror explained that the Mexican farmhand worked for him, and that he didn't speak English very well and that he thought he was attempting to tell the court that his wife was pregnant and was expecting to have the baby the next day. The courtroom crowd exploded with laughter again.

Judge Sullivan gaveled the crowd to order once again and then, with his usual dry sense of humor, said this: "Well, I'm going to excuse him. In either event, he really needs to be there."

After another explosion of laughter from the crowd, Judge Sullivan restored order in the courtroom and the trial proceeded.

CHAPTER 22

Fuzzy and the Phone "Hello, Did You Call Me?"

Fuzzy Wall hated the sound of silence. Almost as much as he hated hard work. Especially hard, physical farm work. What did he like? Well, most of all Fuzzy loved to lecture. You name the topic, and he would expound upon it. And he'd continue the lecture even if you fell asleep.

But let me back up a minute here, and I'll set the stage for you. It was the spring of 1978, in the rural community of Medicine Mound located in northwest Texas. The small town of Vernon, Texas, is located about twenty-five miles to the east. And the small rural town of Chillicothe is located about fifteen miles to the north.

After the terrible drought and the fiscal depression of the 1930s, World War II, and the invention of tractors, pickups, and farm machinery, the rural population had thinned considerably. After all, a tractor could plow a lot more acres in one day than a man and a mule could plow in two weeks.

By 1978, I was forty-two years old; had been raised on a ranch near the Medicine Mound community; had graduated from high school, college, and law school; and had returned home and opened a law office in Vernon. Then I purchased my own small ranch in the Medicine Mound area that I named the Warriors Hollow Ranch.

Fuzzy was about forty-five years old then. Had graduated from high school. Then he retired. He returned to the Medicine Mound community in the early 1970s and had moved into a shack on a small farm owned by his older, hardworking, straitlaced brother, Marteen Wall. Marteen was married to Mildred. Fuzzy and Marteen's parents were also hardworking, straitlaced small-farm owners: Raymond and Elah Wall were Medicine Mound pioneers. Their son Fuzzy was an apple that had fallen a very long way from that apple tree.

In the late spring, while Fuzzy was living in that shack on Marteen's farm—when Fuzzy would ordinarily have been out and about, sometimes even plowing Marteen's fields—it rained. Rained just about every day for a month.

With all that rain and no work to do, and no car to take him somewhere else, Fuzzy was stranded by himself—well, almost by himself. Fortunately (or unfortunately, if you were Marteen) there was a telephone in the shack—in Marteen's name, of course. So every evening Fuzzy would have a sip or two, and then he would come down with an irresistible urge to visit. He'd pick up the phone and call about everybody he knew and talk and talk and talk. And a whole lot of those folks he was visiting with over the telephone did not have an area code that even vaguely resembled Marteen's area code. Before cell phones, long-distance calls could run up your phone bills pretty quickly; and along about then Fuzzy had a semi-girlfriend who had moved to Chicago, and Fuzzy would get his own personalized Chicago weather report nearly every night.

And it came to pass about the first of the next month, the postman came by Marteen's house in town and presented him with what almost proved to have caused Marteen to have a fatal coronary attack. It was an envelope that had a return address attributed to Southwestern Bell Telephone Company. If memory serves, it mentioned a figure of something like eight hundred dollars plus. It has been said (although I personally never believed a word of it) that Marteen's wife, Mildred, made discreet inquiries as to the availability of a reliable hit man shortly thereafter.

Marteen knew he had to take decisive action to avert total bankruptcy—and a divorce. His solution was to buy a big old cast-iron box with a padlock on it. Next morning, he came out from town to the farm and locked up his telephone, disremembering to give Fuzzy a key.

Well, that worked…for maybe a day or two.

After hearing all about the story, I would wait till about midnight, then I'd call Fuzzy and let the phone ring and ring and ring and ring…going into convulsions all the while, imagining the pure agony Fuzzy was going through while trying to claw his way into that iron box. Finally, I'd hang up, take my phone off the hook, roll over, and go to sleep.

Fuzzy absolutely could not stand to think that *somebody* was trying to talk to him and he couldn't get at that damn phone! He could just *smell* it. But couldn't get to it. It drove him absolutely nuts. Bonkers. What did he do? Well, Fuzzy went out in the middle of the night, cranked up Marteen's old pickup, burned Marteen's gas, and drove over to Chillicothe, where he located the nearest phone booth. He put in his dime and started calling everybody he could think of—local and long distance. He said, "Did you just try to call me? Did you just try to call me?" Even if they didn't, he felt obligated to stop and visit for fifteen minutes or so just so's they wouldn't feel slighted. And, of course, he didn't pay for any of the long-distance calls—he simply instructed the operator to charge the call to his "home phone." Whose phone? Whose "home phone"? You guessed it.

Marteen was back to square one!

CHAPTER 23

The Great American Goat-Buying Expedition And Some Very Strange Sidebars Along the Way

Wall-to-wall hijinks. Just one misadventure right after another was the way this caper played out.

The whole thing had seemed simple enough, at least to begin with: We'd just hook a trailer onto my pickup truck, drive down south for a while until we found somebody with some goats for sale, buy a few, load 'em up, and head for home. Then bingo, we'd be feasting on barbecued cabrito.

But then, nothing having anything to do with Fuzzy—Fuzzy Wall—ever turned out to be that simple or easy, especially if it involved travel or money. Particularly other people's money, which was the kind Fuzzy preferred to spend. I knew all that. So it was definitely my fault for even paying any attention to him when he started talking about cabrito.

As I recollect, it was one sunny Saturday afternoon in early spring, and it must have been about 1977. It had been a long winter, and we had a bad case of cabin fever. Anyhow, we were all sitting on the back porch of my cabin out on the ranch sipping a few cool brews while visions of juicy barbecued cabrito danced in our brains and teased our taste buds.

The talking, such as it was, consisted mostly of a monologue conducted by Fuzzy and directed vaguely toward Sweet Child and me. We called him that—Sweet Child—on account of he was only about twenty then and still had a cherubic baby-fat face. His dad, Johnny Koonce, a good friend of mine, was a captain in the Texas Department of Public Safety, working in the narcotics section, and he had investigated a number of drug cases that I had prosecuted while serving as district attorney of the three-county Forty-sixth Judicial District Court in West Texas from 1968 through 1976.

Sweet Child had been out of high school for a couple of years, and having lost whatever little enthusiasm he ever had for higher education, and having nothing better to do, was killing time hanging out at my ranch. Occasionally, but not too often, I even talked him into patching a fence or going to town for groceries or supplies.

But back to my story.

"Cabrito is the best barbecue meat anywhere," Fuzzy continued.

And he went on and on about the exact way you have to kill, bleed, dress, and hang the goat carcass for a while and then marinate it, and just how to barbecue it. Of course, Fuzzy—a self-appointed and anointed professor—never met a subject that he didn't qualify on as a world-class expert, at least according to him. I might add, Fuzzy, then forty, lived in a shack on his brother's farm down the road a few miles.

"Well, you can't buy cabrito around here anywhere," I finally got in edgewise, adding, "I doubt there's a goat within a hundred miles."

"Why, I expect we could just hook up your trailer and take off down south somewhere and find us a few goats in a day or so," said Fuzzy, his enthusiasm completely undiminished by such a minor problem.

Sweet Child chimed in. "We ain't got much anything better to do around here."

"However," I pointed out, "my beat-up trailer is in such bad shape I doubt I could haul jackrabbits in it."

"Goats don't weigh hardly nothing," said Fuzzy. "That ole trailer is plenty good enough for goats."

"Except," I said, "for having a rotten floor, no taillights, and four flat tires, all slick as a baby's butt, and I got no idea where the spare went—except for all that, it *is* in pretty good shape."

"Why, I know where the spare is," Fuzzy cheerfully volunteered. "I borrowed it last winter sometime. Clean forgot. Anyway, we can pick up the spare over at my place on the way out."

"Yeah, and you don't have *real* flats on them tires," Sweet Child explained. "It's just a few of them got little mesquite thorn punctures—just slow leaks. I'll go get the compressor and air 'em up right now, and we can just stop now and again at some gas station and keep 'em pumped up."

"I'll just go right in and fix us up some sandwiches and ice down the beer," chimed in Fuzzy.

"We probably only need to get twenty or thirty head. That'll be plenty," Sweet Child observed.

So that's how it went, and the next thing I knew we were headed south—me and Fuzzy and Sweet Child—in my old red Ford ranch pickup pulling the afore-described old beat-up open-top sixteen-foot stock trailer.

And, I must admit, our garb was a shade on the bizarre side, although I thought it strangely appropriate for this kind of expedition.

I was the most conservatively dressed, wearing ordinary Levi's, boots, a western shirt, a leather vest, and what Fuzzy called my "Kansas-City-go-to-hell" hat, which in truth was the kind of high-crown, flat-brim hat that old Tom Mix used to wear in those old-timey Westerns—if anybody but me can remember Tom Mix anymore or what kind of hat he wore. Anyway, you can look at the picture.

Sweet Child wore a black derby hat and generally looked like those old pictures of Butch Cassidy or the Sundance Kid, I forget which.

Fuzzy's costume, of course, was marvelously tasteless—garish and bizarre to boot. Fuzzy was about five foot five and probably didn't weigh more than 110 pounds. His costume on the trip consisted of tattered cutoff Levi's that exposed his skinny bird legs, encased in high-top cowboy boots with spurs, a short-sleeve red T-shirt, and a big old straw cowboy hat. As an added touch, he wore Hollywood-style sunglasses, all of which was topped off with a god-awful, ankle-length fur coat that was so old and patchy I never could figure out what kind of animal it had once graced. Plus, a toy sheriff's badge—a real fashion statement there, folks.

Members of the great American goat-buying expedition standing (L-R) Bill Neal, Murrell "Fuzzy" Wall, and Kenny "Sweet Child" Koonce and the worn goat hauling trailer, circa 1977.

So off we went, headed south, but on account of the entire tire pumping and fixing up it took to get us on the road, we didn't make much headway that day. In fact, it was getting dark by the time we got to the little town of Benjamin. But, we had a good friend there, Sheriff H. C. Stone, who had often come out to my ranch to enjoy some of the impromptu barbecues and executive staff meetings we referred to as the "Knox County executive law enforcement conferences."

So, we stopped at the old county jail where the sheriff lived. And, perhaps on account of knowing us pretty well, he never blinked when I explained we were on an official goat-buying expedition, heading somewhere south—just exactly where to we hadn't yet decided—and thought we might just spend the night with him in the jail.

Fuzzy piped up and said, "Well, H. C., we figure we're going to end up in jail sometime or another before this here expedition is over with, so we might just as well get all that over with right off the bat."

Sheriff Stone, who for some reason always thought Fuzzy was hilarious, broke up on that observation, and, shaking his head, led us back to our jail accommodations. As an added courtesy, he didn't even bother to lock us up that night. Next morning, he fed us with the rest of the jailbirds, and then off we went again heading, vaguely, southward. But we didn't see any goats all day long.

That night we ended up way out west in Alpine, Texas, where, not too many years before, Hollywood had filmed the sensational hit movie *Giant* close by. Since we didn't know the sheriff down there, we were forced to put up in a motel. The Ramada, if I recall right. Anyway, it was a pretty nice motel and had a nice cocktail bar, which we immediately invaded, having made a long and tiresome journey pulling that old trailer and having to stop just about every other little town to keep the tires pumped up.

It's just a downright strange thing how folks don't want to believe you when you tell the truth, but will fall for some totally outlandish, off-the-wall tale. Well, that was the way it was that night at the crowded motel cocktail bar. I guess our outlandish garb must have really aroused the crowd's curiosity, because it wasn't long before several locals were over at our table, just busting to know what the hell we were up to. I explained that we were on a goat-buying trip. But they weren't buying *that* ridiculous story!

Finally, some of them said, "I'll bet you guys are down here to shoot another Hollywood movie, aren't you?"

Well, that was the *wrong* thing to say to Fuzzy. That punched his button, and he was off and running, confessing that really and truly that *was* what we were doing there.

I don't recollect what all he told them, but it was a lot. Something, I think, about we were going to shoot a sequel to *Giant*, and he was going to play Jet Rink's long-lost half-brother showing up to claim his interest in the oil patch action and drill more wildcat oil wells, etc., etc., etc., explaining that Elizabeth Taylor was going to fall in love with him in his version. They swallowed all that malarkey hook, line, and sinker, and the more they believed, the wilder Fuzzy's stories got. The good part was that they started buying us drinks.

The next day, we decided to take off a day from our goat search and do a little tour of the Big Bend. While we didn't know the sheriff in Alpine, we did know Ken Akin, who, like Sweet Child's dad, was then an undercover narcotics agent for the Texas Department of Public Safety, or DPS, stationed there. He, like Sweet Child's father, had also been stationed in North Texas and had helped prepare some dope cases that I had prosecuted. He and I and Sweet Child's dad, Johnny Koonce (who was at that time stationed at El Paso), were all good friends, so we looked up Ken. He was busy that day but promised to meet us at Presidio the next evening and we would go across the river to Ojinaga, Mexico, and check out the nightlife.

Having the day to kill, we decided to go down to the town of Terlingua, which at that time was almost a ghost town. Look around there and then come back up the Rio Grande road through Lajitas and on to Presidio to meet Ken. But along the way we took an interesting side diversion at the old trading post at Terlingua. We got to the trading post in the early afternoon. The country down there is desolate, but with its own eerie charm. Nobody was at the trading post, except two old geezers who were minding the store. Though it was early afternoon, the old coots had already worked up a pretty good glow—both were lounging on a bench on the front porch of the trading post, beers in hand. So, of course, Fuzzy immediately started visiting with them. Fuzzy never met a stranger.

We even took some pictures on the front porch, as you can see. One picture shows me and Sweet Child with one of the old coots in the middle.

Taking it easy on the front porch of a Terlingua Trading Post, Terlingua, Texas. (L-R) Kenny "Sweet Child" Koonce, unidentified old coot, and Bill Neal, circa 1977.

After a while I was beginning to get bored with all this chatter between Fuzzy and the old coots inside the trading post, and so I wandered off in the direction of the front door. For some reason, one of the old coots broke away from his buddy and Fuzzy and came over to me. By this time, I was standing in the doorway.

I don't recall exactly what he said, but I think it was a question about what we were doing down there. Now, bear in mind, we were only a stone's throw from Mexico and trainloads of dope were being smuggled across the border.

For some reason, boredom mainly, I had an inspiration. I figured that the old coot, being a native there, knew the dope scene and the players. Also, he just *looked* like a character of questionable moral fiber, to put it mildly. The conversation went something like this:

> ME: Man, I dunno. *(I shook my head and tried to look a little desperate.)* Got my problems.

OC: Yeah?
ME: Sure 'nuf. A big, big one.
OC: Hey, yeah. Whassa deal?
ME: Hell, I don't need to be *talking* about it—know what I mean?
OC: Problems with the Man [read "the law"]?
ME: Worse, man, worse.
OC: Hey, man. I know lots of folks down here—know everybody. Maybe I can put you in touch. I mean I know all the *right* people down here.
ME: I dunno. I just don't need to be *talking*. Like, I don't *know* these people down here. I don't need to be talking to the wrong people.
OC: I can *tell* you who to talk to.

By this time, he had already lowered his voice to a whisper and was in my face. He could just smell that money.

ME: Man, I guess I got no choice. I'm in a world of shit, and that ain't no lie.
OC: Yeah?
ME: You see that trailer out there? *(Pointing to my stock trailer.)*
OC: Yeah.
ME: *(getting right in his face—almost touching noses and whispering, with as much desperation in my whisper as I could manage)* Well, I'm supposed to have that damned trailer loaded with grass and be back in New Jersey by Friday, man. And you know what, I can't find my contact. Been here two damned days and he hasn't showed. But see, here's the rub. See, these big people—I mean big, big people in Jersey—are fronting. I mean I got a bundle of cash. I don't show Friday with the shit or the cash, I mean it ain't gonna be

> pretty, know where I'm coming from? See, like, I had to front a good chunk of their cash to *my* contacts. So now I ain't *got* all their money. And I ain't got *any* grass, and here I am, ripped off and deep in shit!
>
> OC: Hey, I can *do it* for you, man! I know the *right* people. You just don't know how much stuff comes across down through the park, man. Tons, man, tons.
>
> Me: Hey, I gotta do something. And do it now! I mean, can you handle *that much*? You know, hell, a couple hundred pounds ain't gonna do me no good. I gotta do big. Can you, you know, do big? I mean really big?

I'm doing my best to keep from breaking up, but I'm noticing out of the corner of my eye that the other old coot who had been talking to Fuzzy was only about twenty feet away and was beginning to pay attention to our face-to-face whispering conversation. He began to move closer and finally he was really paying very close attention and ignoring Fuzzy's nonsense. I saw in his eyes some alarm bells were going off. Finally, he eased up to his buddy and me and kept trying to get his attention. But my old coot was too caught up in this heavy-duty drug deal to notice him.

> OC: Shit, man, you talking to the dude that can do this deal!
>
> Me: I dunno, man. It's gotta be big and done right *now*! You just don't, you know, look like you could do that *heavy* a deal.
>
> OC: Shit, man. Trust me, I know the *big* players down here—can put you in touch now, just so you take care of me when it comes down.

Now the other old coot was close enough to hear us and thus verify his worst suspicions. He had given up trying to make warning signals to his buddy. He was now pulling on his buddy's sleeve. But to no avail. My old coot was into it big time. His friend finally grabbed him by the arm and bodily dragged him away. Fuzzy and Sweet Child couldn't figure out what was going on. I saw Fuzzy's old coot whispering to my old coot and gesturing toward me. I could even see his mouth forming the word: "Narc! Narc!"

I nodded at Fuzzy and Sweet Child and we drifted out to the pickup and got in. About the time I got the pickup started, here came both the old coots. By now Fuzzy's old coot had convinced my old coot that I really was "the man" and that he was about to be trapped.

They both came charging out to the pickup. I was in the driver's seat with the window down. They were the picture of outraged self-righteousness.

> OC: I know'd you bastard was a damned narc all the time.
> Me: Really?
> OC: Yeah, and now let me tell you what we do to damned narcs down here in this country.

I slowly motioned for Sweet Child to open the glove compartment and hand me my pistol. It was only a little old .22, but it *looked* big. It was a six-shooter revolver and it had a thick, six-inch barrel. So Sweet Child pulled it out and slipped it to me. I came up with it right in their faces.

> Me: Well, let me tell you what *we* do to damn dope peddlers up in my country!

As they wheeled around and cut a high trail, I fired off a couple of rounds straight up. The last I saw of those two old coots they probably were hooking 'em up faster than they had in fifty years—one disappeared around one corner of the trading post and the other shot around the other corner. We departed that place, in a spray of gravel, laughing all the way to Presidio.

*****

Late that afternoon, as planned, we met Ken Akin, in Presidio—and also a most attractive and gracious young Mexican American lady, Delia Juarez, who worked at her mother's travel agency in downtown Presidio. I had met Delia about a year earlier when I was in her neck of the woods representing a civil client on a cattle importation matter. Delia and I had hit it off right from the get-go and I had kept in touch. When we ended up in Alpine the day before, I decided to forget goats and focus on Delia.

We were also looking forward to a reunion with our old buddy Ken, and so everybody was in a get-down celebrating mood, and we made the most of it. We all went over to Ojinaga and, with Delia as our guide and translator, and Fuzzy as our front man, I reckon we must have met and visited with most everybody in Ojinaga.

When we finally got through visiting and celebrating in Ojinaga about two in the morning, we all came back across the river to Presidio. Sweet Child, Fuzzy, and Ken decided they had had enough celebrating and so took off in Ken's car and headed for Alpine. I told them I'd be along directly, and we'd meet at the same motel in Alpine where we'd spent the last night. Delia and I continued the celebration. About an hour later we pulled up to the house where Delia lived with her mother. It was a great big old house surrounded by an adobe wall—kind of a compound. It was obvious that these folks weren't sharecroppers. In fact, Delia's mother was a widow who owned a high-toned travel agency in downtown Presidio. So, there I was entering the stockade at three in the morning in my pickup, goat trailer attached, and Delia in tow. It was about an hour later when we concluded our visit and I headed toward Alpine.

The map said it was about ninety miles from Presidio to Alpine, but that night it seemed to be at least five hundred miles to Alpine. I thought I would never get there, and my eyelids were made of cast iron. Somehow, though, I did arrive just as the first hint of dawn was dissolving the darkness. My thoughts were on nothing except a soft bed. But that wasn't to be—at least not until after I had yet another very exciting and most sobering misadventure, the humor of which only occurred to me in retrospect.

The thing was that, what with so much celebrating going on, I somehow had assumed—incorrectly as it turned out—that Fuzzy and Sweet Child would be in the *same room* in that Alpine motel where we'd spent the last night.

I knocked on that door about to collapse with exhaustion. Nothing happened. I knocked again. Nothing happened. I thought, "These turkeys are playing a game with me." I banged on the door vigorously. Nothing happened. I ran out of patience then. I vigorously banged on the door again and hollered, "You damned turkeys, let me in this door or I'm fixin' to kick it in!" Well, that did get some results.

The door opened. I was looking straight ahead—into what, after I focused, strangely enough, appeared to be someone's navel, of all things. Directly, I began to look up, and up, and up and up, until it seemed like I was looking straight up…into the face of about the biggest guy I had ever seen, and definitely not a face I had ever seen before. And it definitely was not smiling down at me.

And I was thinking, *Lordy, I sure hope this is not fixin' to turn into a total disaster!* Not being able to come up with anything better, I just turned away, shrugged, and started walking off, saying, "Oh, well, hell, just forget it!" I tell you, though, I was listening mighty hard for the sound of bare feet behind me while tensed and ready to break the world's one-hundred-yard dash record. But finally, I heard the door close. Whew! What a relief! Suddenly I was not a bit sleepy anymore.

The next day we got an early start—right after lunch, that is. And since we were out in that neck of the woods, we decided to postpone our goat hunt a while longer and go on over to El Paso, where my friend, and Sweet Child's dad, Johnny Koonce, was then stationed. So we headed west.

Johnny and his wife, Della, lived in a big apartment complex. We rolled in late the next afternoon, and just as we were pulling up to their apartment house, I cut a corner a little short and the damned trailer wheel rammed into the curb, and that resulted in a bent axle. Some smart aleck was standing around taking it all in, and he yelled, "Hey, you bent your axle!"

I yelled back, "Don't worry about it—hell, it'll grow back." Then we finally arrived at the Koonce home.

It took two or three days for us to get reorganized and repair the axle. I must add that Della, probably thc most gracious and forbearing hostess in history, never missed a lick or batted an eye at the invasion by our motley crew that included her son, Sweet Child. While Johnny was working during the day, she took us on a supervised shopping tour of Juarez.

Having finally gotten reorganized, we all slept until about noon the next day and then hit the road again and decided it was time to get serious about this goat business. So, we headed on up north into New Mexico. Our goat expert, Fuzzy, authoritatively advised us that there would be plenty of goats up that direction. (I don't think he'd ever been near that place in his whole life.) We went on over, passed through Carlsbad, and went on north without seeing goat one. But then we got lucky. Well, sort of. We ran into Leroy.

We stopped at this little bar out in the country. I mean it was desolate country out there, deserted sand hills and such, and this little bar was in the middle of nowhere. Nothing around it but sand hills. And sagebrush. And eternity. If I recollect right, it was somewhere south of Artesia. Somewhere out there. We were parched and discouraged, since we had yet to see one goat. So, we pulled over at this little bar to console ourselves, and there encountered a few grizzled natives. And Leroy.

Naturally, after a beer or two, the bar patrons were curious as to what such a weird group was doing out in that remote country. They hadn't seen anything like us in quite a spell. If ever. No use trying to explain to those old hard cases we were going to make some kind of a movie. So, for lack of anything better to say, I just told the truth. "We're looking for some meat goats to buy."

"Well, now you're looking at just the right feller to help you out," said Leroy. Somehow, I just knew this was not going to be easy—or quick. No doubt about it, I was dealing with a real goat trader here. Sensing my disadvantage, I glanced around to my companions and hoped for support. But I should have known better. I saw that Sweet Child was totally focused on his cold beverage while Fuzzy was totally focused on the cold beverage server, who was not all that bad looking either. I could see that my compadres were not going to be any help at all. I was strictly on my own.

"Well," I began, "you know, I have a little fresh pasture and room for a few more goats to add to my herd, and, you know, I thought if I could pick up some real bargains I might just go on ahead."

"What kind you lookin' for?"

"What I could use is six or eight good young Spanish nannies with kids ready to wean. But real good stuff, as I have worked hard to breed a quality herd."

"Gotcha," said Leroy. And I thought to myself, *I imagine you're right about that!* "I got all kinds of goats," Leroy added.

But I said, "Well, what were you thinking about asking for your nannies, Leroy?"

"Oh, I dunno. I'd sure be fair with you on it, all right. What were you looking to pay for the right kind—like I got?"

"Well, of course, I'd sure have to look at them, but, like, what ballpark are we playing in here?" I said. To tell you the truth, I didn't have the foggiest notion of what the market was on goats. I thought if I could get Leroy to name a price, I could start bargaining from there. I figured it was going to be about twice what the market actually was. But Leroy wasn't having any of that. I just knew it wasn't going to be easy.

"I'll tell you what," said Leroy, "you take that napkin there and I'll take this one here, and you write on your napkin what you would give for such a good nanny as we are talking about, and I'll write on mine what I would take, and then we'll turn over at the same time and see how far apart we are. And then, you know, we can go on from there."

"Well," I said, "I guess that might work as a starter."

"Okay," he said, "here goes." And he scribbled something on his napkin. I wrote something on my napkin. Then we turned 'em over.

As it turned out we both wrote the exact same thing on our napkins, which was: "F— you." At least, that broke the ice. After Leroy and I and the other old geezers who by now were taking a lively interest in the proceedings, quit laughing and regained our composure somewhat, Leroy bought me a cold beverage. Then we proceeded with the negotiations, although I had won—or at least tied—round one. I had convinced Leroy that, at least, I was not a teetotal greenhorn fool. Close, maybe, but not tee-totally.

This went on all afternoon. I began to realize that being a big-time goat trader was not as easy as it might appear to the uninitiated. This was hard work. After a while I said, "By the way, Leroy, I have been out of touch with things for a while. I was wondering if you happened to catch the goat market the past few days?"

"Why, the last I heard it was pretty strong. I expect it may be up several dollars a head what with the shortage of goats nowadays."

"Well now, maybe before we go any farther, I had better check with my partner. He keeps up with the market every day, and I'd never hear the end of it if I was to cough up more than the market."

Without further ado I got up and went across the bar to the payphone and called my legal secretary long distance.

"Where in the hell are you, and what in the hell have you been up to?" That was the first thing she said to me.

"Well," I replied, "I'm here now, but I've been all around."

She said a lot of unprintable things then and went on talking about "schedules" and "settings" and clients and lawyers and judges and other dull stuff. I was really shocked to hear her talk with such colorful language. But I said, rather loudly, "What's the goat market done? Yeah, Spanish nannies."

She then wanted to know if there was a responsible adult nearby that she could forward commitment papers to. Since there wasn't, I hung up.

"Leroy," I said, resuming my negotiating chair, "looks like they hit the skids yesterday. Down five to seven dollars a head." The negotiations went on until almost closing time, when we finally struck a deal. At least, it was a "maybe" deal, depending on, first, my inspection and approval of the goats, and second, and before that, we had to catch the goats. According to Leroy, the goats were roaming around out there in the sand hills…somewhere.

I don't recollect what bargain we struck. Seems like twenty-five or thirty-five dollars for the nannies and about half that for a kid. But don't hold me to that. Whatever it was, I'm sure it was considerably above the market. Nevertheless, we had to have some cabrito. Fuzzy assured me.

The next day, we met Leroy at the bar and then went out over those desolate sand hills attempting to find and capture the goats. I don't know which was the hardest, trading for goats or catching them. We ran all over those sand hills and nearly wore ourselves plumb out, but we managed to trap about twenty goats in Leroy's broken-down pens. To say those pens were dilapidated would be a compliment. They were the kind of pens I grew up calling "3B corrals"—shorthand for "Busted boards, bailing wire patched, and By-god-which-way'd-they-go?" We finally penned them. I cut out six or seven nannies and three or four weaning kids, as I recall. I didn't know what I was doing except I picked out the ones that looked like they would be edible. At least after somebody had fed them for a couple of months.

Then I backed up my old trailer to a rickety loading chute and we chased them into the trailer. Leroy was standing there with his hand on my trailer gate, and kind of as an afterthought, I said to Leroy, "By the way, Leroy, you do guarantee you own these goats, don't you?"

And as Leroy slammed my trailer gate shut on the last of the goats, he said to me, "Listen, the only thing I'm guaranteeing about them goats is that they is loaded."

I said, "Well, you know, Leroy, I appreciate that. Just figured I needed some kind of guarantee on those goats." I paid Leroy for the goats and we departed that place and never returned.

We made it to Lubbock about ten o'clock that night and since it was still early, we decided to drop by and see another old friend, B. J. Green, who I had gotten to know when he was a Texas Ranger stationed in Seymour a few years earlier. He was also a good friend of Johnny Koonce's.

When we showed up, B. J. was—to say the least—taken aback by our unexpected arrival, as well as our bedraggled appearance. After having chased those goats over the desert for two or three hours we were not the most handsome sight he'd ever seen—not to mention the odor. But B. J., knowing us, quickly recovered—at least temporarily. After we got in and he poured us a drink, he casually inquired as to what brought us to Lubbock.

"Oh," Fuzzy replied, "we been out buying goats."

"Buying goats?" chuckled B. J. "And probably a few buffaloes and giraffes too."

"No," I said. "No giraffes and no buffaloes, just goats. Wanna see 'em?"

Still thinking it was all a joke, B. J. said, "Well, where are they?"

"Why, B. J., we got them right outside in the trailer."

B. J. took another swallow of whiskey and took a good look at all three of us and said, "Bullshit!"

But when we finally walked out and climbed up on the side of the trailer and looked over the top rail, he gawked a few minutes and muttered, "Well, I'll be damned!" And he took another double shot of whiskey.

When we departed B. J.'s house it was getting close to midnight. I remember that because of the next unexpected misadventure we had. We were still in Lubbock somewhere and I remember it was next to some nightclub, because about the time we went past that club, two things happened: first, it was closing time and a fair crop of bar patrons were emerging from it when I ran over a bump or something in the road right in front of the club; and second, damned if some of the rotten flooring on my trailer didn't finally give way and fall out, along with three or four of the little goats. So we bailed out and started chasing goats in downtown Lubbock. I hollered to Sweet Child to get in the trailer and make sure no more goats escaped.

The good news was that Fuzzy and I attracted enthusiastic help from several tipsy departing club patrons in capturing our goats. They immediately joined in the chase with much gusto. I can still remember one energized drunk staggering after one of the kid goats, hollering, "Look at the baby cheep, look at the baby cheep!"

With all that help, we—after a wild roundup in the city streets of Lubbock—gathered the escaped goats in fairly short order and got them back in the trailer. Sweet Child was still sitting on that hole. We thought about leaving him there since he was doing such a good job. Thinking better of that, however, we finally got the spare tire out and tied it over the hole in the trailer floor and started out toward home.

We proceeded at least as far as Floydada that night. We got there somewhere around three or four in the morning, and we were plumb tuckered out. I knew the local home demonstration agent there. Her name was Sharon Hillis, and she and I had been close friends for a number of years when she was stationed in Hardeman County. Wc stopped by and went roughly through the same routine we had done with B. J. Green earlier—much earlier. Somehow, knowing us, Sharon didn't seem as surprised at our cargo or our appearance as B. J. had been. She invited us into the house and she fixed us some supper (or was it breakfast?), and we immediately cratered. Fuzzy, as was his custom, just fell down on the living room floor, clothes, spurs, and all, and went to sleep. The next morning, he got up, brushed himself off, and observed, "Must have slept pretty light last night; didn't even get a wrinkle in my duds."

Sharon had to go to work that morning, but she wanted us to stay over and made the mistake of saying so. We decided to do just that. We sure did need the rest. Consequently, it was about the middle of the afternoon before we yawned, stretched, and got vertical. Then we took a notion to barbecue one of those goats. We couldn't wait to get a taste of Fuzzy's cabrito. We figured to surprise Sharon when she came home from work. By the time she arrived, we had excavated a pretty good-sized pit in her backyard, had gathered some firewood, and had one of the kids strung up by its heels from the big Elm tree beside the pit. She was very surprised all right…to put it mildly. She looked a little apprehensive at that scene. Then she went inside, and when she came back outside in a few minutes she looked a lot more apprehensive. She kept saying something about her neighbors.

But Fuzzy reassured her. "Why, shoot, Sharon, that ain't no problem. We'll string up two of them goats and invite 'em all over."

Still, that somehow didn't seem to appeal to her, so we filled in a perfectly good barbecue pit and departed. Headed home. We were too tired when we finally got back to my ranch to fool with the goats anymore that night, and that led me to make a big mistake. Instead of just leaving those goats in the trailer like I ought to have, I decided to turn them out in my corrals—cattle corrals. Cattle corrals are not goat-proof corrals. I figured if we put out a tub of water and some feed, the goats would just bed down for the night and we would get up there first thing in the morning and goat-proof the fences. That's what I figured, but it didn't work out that way.

When we got up the next morning and walked up to the corrals...well, sure enough, the corrals were as solitary as a cemetery. All the goats were gone! And I have not seen any of those goats to this very day. Gone down to the Pease River breaks, no doubt, and the coyotes had a feast on unbarbecued cabrito.

Lucky for us, we ate some cabrito when we were in Juarez.

The next Saturday, when Fuzzy came over, and before he could begin his lecture, I said, "You know, Fuzzy, what I sure would like to have today is some good old barbecued pork ribs."

In fact, I'd have settled for a peanut butter sandwich—I'd been barbecued myself all the past week by my secretary and several disgruntled clients. And all that was mild compared to the barbecuing I got from the judge.

CHAPTER 24

The Mayor of Birmingham, Texas—That's Me! A Frontier Land Scam

One day as I was walking down the hall of the Hardeman County courthouse, a lady I had never seen before confronted me. She seemed rather indignant as she approached. With hands on hips she demanded to know if my name was Bill Neal. When I admitted that I was Bill Neal, she announced that I was trespassing on land that she owned in Hardeman County. As it turned out, the land in question was part of the ranch I owned along the Kansas City, Missouri, and Orient Railroad south of Medicine Mound and near the Pease River. At that point she held up a land deed that was dated 1910 conveying land to her grandfather, which included some city lots in the town of Birmingham, Texas. She explained that she was from the eastern part of the United States and had recently inherited those city lots from her grandfather and demanded that I take her to Birmingham so she could view her lots. If she had been a nice lady, I would have been sorry to disillusion her.

As we stood in the hallway, I attempted to explain to her that there was no such place as Birmingham, Texas. The creation of Birmingham, Texas, was all a part of an early-day land scam, and her grandfather apparently was one of the 393 Easterners who had been suckered into buying lots in a town that never existed. They did, however, receive a deed that was recorded in the Hardeman County Deed Records in 1910 that actually did convey the city lots sold to the new owners. The scam artist had actually had the nonexistent town of Birmingham surveyed into city lots and streets and filed the survey in the county deed records, so when he sold a city lot he would have a description of an actual piece of land.

J. M. "Jess" Christie was the scam artist who had persuaded some folks back in the eastern states that with the coming of railroads in the American West, it would soon be populated by thriving towns and villages along the railroad tracks and their property would soon be very valuable. Meanwhile, when he purchased the tracts of land, he told the rancher a very different story. He told him that this land would be a good shipping point along the railroad to market area ranchers' cattle.

When he sold the city lots to the folks back East, he showed them a lithograph that depicted Birmingham as the land of milk and honey. It was an elaborate picture that supposedly showed downtown Birmingham, as well as the surrounding area and the Pease River in the background. Birmingham was depicted as a thriving young town with schools, churches, businesses, houses, and, of course, the railroad running through it, the depot, and grain elevators, with many people traveling up and down the streets. The surrounding area was depicted as very flat, fertile farming country, with rich crops of corn, wheat, oats, and cotton growing in the fields and a lot of plantation-style farm homes dotting the landscape. Up and down the rural lanes, farmers were busily hauling their crops to town while others were traveling the roads in smart horse-drawn buggies. But the most startling thing was that the Pease River could be seen in the background looking like a very large flowing river with blue water, and, of all things, a very large steamboat was coursing the deep waters of the mighty Pease. In actuality, the Pease River was and still is a shallow stream about ankle deep at best and colored by the red clay riverbed.

As it turned out, this was a popular scam during the time railroads were being constructed in the American West. And various scammers were selling city lots to folks back East in nonexistent towns that began popping up all along the railroad.

I explained to the lady that none of the owners of city lots in Birmingham had ever erected a home, built a business, or made any use of the land. Since that time, several ranchers had owned, fenced off, and used the entire 640-acre section of land that encompassed Birmingham, Texas, and had also paid ad valorem taxes on the same land.

Finally, I attempted to explain to the woman that there is a Texas law called Adverse Possession. And that although the original deed given to her grandfather actually conveyed the city lots to him, nevertheless, she had lost title to her land under the provisions of that law which provides that if you fence off, possess, and use a tract of land, continuously and adversely to the record owner for more than ten years, you acquire legal title to the tract of land yourself.

As the lady began to realize that she had not actually inherited land in Birmingham, Texas, she slowly turned and quietly left the courthouse. And that is how I became the mayor and sole inhabitant of Birmingham, Texas.

CHAPTER 25

Me and Aunt Olga
In the Oil Patch and the Courtroom

One day in the late 1970s, a lady marched into my law office—no appointment, mind you—and announced that her name was Olga Barrett and that she had decided that I would represent her. "Just call me Aunt Olga," she said.

Olga was a widow and lived in Abilene, Texas. She was in the oil business and wanted to acquire oil and gas leases covering several thousand acres of land in northwest Foard County, Texas. I was well acquainted with that part of the country, being a native and having previously served as district attorney for the tri-county area that included Foard County. In my private law practice, I had represented numerous citizens in the area, including a number of landowners. I agreed to represent her in her business dealings.

*****

I'll never forget one of my first missions with Aunt Olga. She insisted that I accompany her to Houston. Our mission: acquiring an oil and gas lease from the owner of a fractional mineral interest then owned by a man named Paul Tucker. Of course, neither Aunt Olga nor I had ever met Paul. Turned out he was a practicing lawyer in downtown Houston.

We walked into Paul Tucker's office. Aunt Olga introduced herself and me to Paul, who was seated at his desk. She told Paul that she knew he owned a mineral interest in the Foard County land and that she was an oil and gas operator, and she wanted to obtain an oil and gas lease from him. Told him her offer price, then produced the oil and gas lease, walked over to the side of his desk, and laid the lease before him pointing out the signature line at the bottom of the page. She said, "Sign right here." Paul picked up the lease and began reading it.

"No need bothering to read it," she announced. "Bill Neal here is a top-notch lawyer. He graduated top of his class at UT law school. Just sign right here."

Paul Tucker, it turned out, was a friendly and easygoing fellow. He smiled at Aunt Olga's order and said, "Oh, I don't reckon it'll take me long to look it over." He looked back over Aunt Olga's shoulder at me, then smiled and winked. Paul did read over the oil and gas lease that I had prepared, and shortly thereafter did execute it and received his bonus money check.

Paul and I became good friends and remain so to this day. In fact, he has visited me several times on my ranch and we have been on a number of quail hunts together.

*****

There had not been much oil and gas activity in the area for several years, but now some oil and gas companies had begun sending "land men" into the area to acquire oil and gas leases from the landowners in Foard County.

I had previously represented a number of oil companies in examining land titles, preparing oil leases, and negotiating with landowners. But much to my surprise, Olga Barrett was not representing an oil exploration company—she *was* the company.

Ms. Barrett had been in the oil business since 1953, as a partner with her husband, Arnold, until his death in 1975, and then on her own for a few years. Until Arnold's death they were responsible for drilling 250 wildcats and field development wells in the west central Texas area. She later commented that she knew how to read well logs and she knew exactly what she was looking for in a good drilling prospect. She was quoted in the *Abilene Reporter-News* as saying, "An oil producer is someone who can do more than sell a deal. It is someone who knows a good prospect, buys the leases, raises the money, drills a well in a workmanlike manner, and knows how to complete a well and how to produce. In my book it's someone who puts his own money into a project, too. That's what I do and why I'm a producer."

Duchess of the oil patch, Olga Barrett, shown on the cover of a booklet introducing Olga as a petroleum producer in West Texas, March 1979.

That's exactly what Olga Barrett did next when she undertook to purchase a large block of oil leases covering several thousand acres in northwest Foard County. However, there was one landowner, Hartley Easley, a crusty old rancher, who refused to lease his Foard County ranchland to Olga.

Olga next concocted a unique and inventive plan of how to market the leasehold acreage. She divided the acreage into a checkerboard pattern with each tract containing eighty acres. Olga retained exclusive title to half the eighty-acre checkerboarded tracts and sold all the remaining tracts in this same area to a company called Corpening Enterprises from Fort Worth, Texas. Olga's agreement required

Corpening Enterprises to drill the first well on one of their checkerboarded tracks and provide her with all drilling, completion, and production information. Such drilling information would be very useful to Olga if she drilled an adjacent well on one of her eighty-acre tracts.

The agreement also provided, however, that if Olga did later buy a lease from Hartley Easley for his land that was within the acreage she had purchased, she would then offer to sell and convey to Corpening Enterprises half of the land she had acquired.

In 1978, Corpening did drill the first well in one of its tracts and it was a gusher named the Thompson No. 1. This well was located on land in the northwest corner of Section 23 adjacent to the Easley unleased land. It thus became apparent that the southeast quarter of Section 23 was extremely valuable, since an offset well could be drilled near the Thompson well. Unfortunately for Olga, that unleased land was still owned by Hartley Easley.

CHECKERBOARD ACREAGE OF BARRETT & CORPENING OIL LEASES

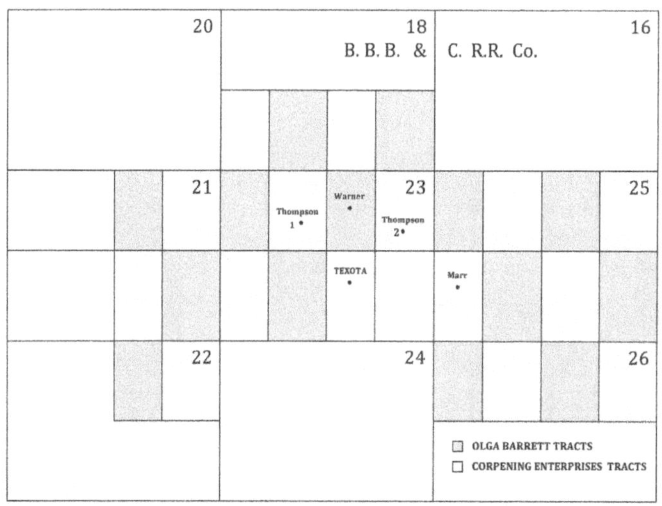

Fig. 4. Map of the Foard County Checker boarded eighty-acre oil leases owned by Olga Barrett and Corpening Enterprises.

*****

Even though Aunt Olga was a petite lady with blonde hair, when it came to doing business she was very forceful. She barked at people like a Marine drill sergeant giving orders to his recruits. When that didn't work, she sometimes resorted to her submissive persona: "the poor mistreated little wider lady." One time an Abilene drilling company had repeatedly sent Olga bills for drilling mud it had furnished her in drilling a well. But instead of sending a payment to them, Olga sent them a letter with a picture drawn by her doctor illustrating a heart problem that she was having. When the drilling mud company received Olga's letter containing the picture of her heart and no check, the frustrated owner of the company then forwarded a response to Olga also containing a picture. The mud company's president removed his pants and underwear, sat on a copy machine, and took a picture. Included with the photo was this response: "We are sorry to hear about your heart problem, but as far as we are concerned you are just a pain in our ass, a picture of which is enclosed." That was one time when Olga's tactic of switching personas didn't work.

*****

Meanwhile, Olga learned that Corpening Enterprises had drilled the highly productive Thompson No. 1 well, adjacent to the unleased quarter section of land still owned by Hartley Easley. She had failed to get a lease from Easley because her overbearing personality did not appeal to that crusty old rancher. But that didn't deter Olga. She was determined to obtain a lease on that land somehow. So Olga and David Hooper, her lawyer in Abilene, devised a plan.

First, Hooper and Olga hired a man named Franklin Coufal to take the lease in the name of Texota Corporation. And Franklin Coufal did just that. He purchased an oil and gas lease on Easley's land for thirty-six thousand dollars. Hooper had recently organized the Texota Corporation. He was the president, and he and his wife, Christine May, were the sole stockholders. David had organized Texota for the purpose of disguising that Olga would become the beneficial owner of the Hartley Easley lease. In fact, Olga Barrett furnished the funds Hooper used to acquire the lease for Texota on March 14, 1979, and five days later Olga wrote this letter to Scott Corpening, one of the brothers owning Corpening Enterprises:

Re: Section Nos. 23, 21, 25, 26, and
22, Blk A, T & N O RR Co.
Survey, Foard County, Texas

Dear Scott,

In compliance with our conversation of last week relative to the operations of the acreage in Section Nos. 23, 21, 25, 26, and 22, I would like to be the Operator of these leases in this area since I am the largest interest holder.

I will keep you and your investors well informed at all times. The drilling, completion, and operation of the wells will be done professionally and by professionals. Scott, I will be happy to work with you and your investors. In fact, it will be an honor to work with you.

I have been approached by Texota Oil Company (of Houston, I think) for a farm-out of a part of my checkerboarded acreage. I was told that they recently obtained a lease covering the Easley 160-acre tract in the Southeast Quarter of Section No. 23.

I told them I would be interested in a farm-out from them of their 160-acre tract and I was promised a letter of agreement early next week.

Yours very truly,
Olga Barrett

*****

When Scott Corpening failed to reply to Olga's letter, she then wrote the following letter to him dated May 1, 1979:

Re: SE ¼ of Sec. No. 23, T & N O RR.
And Sec. No. 16, BBB & C RR. Co.

Surveys, Foard Co., Texas—800 acres more or less

Dear Scott,

Texota of Houston, Texas has approached me to trade with me on some of my acreage and on the above captioned acreage.

As you know, I was not able to lease the Easley acreage in this area.

I asked Texota what kind of a trade they wanted on their acreage. They said they wanted to sell one-half interest of 75% revenue interest in said acreage for $1,000,000. The front money is $200,000 consisting of bonuses, commission, abstracts, title opinion, legal fees, etc. The $400,000 per well is to drill and complete a well located in the northwest corner of Section No. 23, and to drill and complete a well located in the southwest corner of Section No. 16. If it does not take that much money to drill and complete these wells then whatever is remaining will be refunded to whoever buys this prospect from them. They have chosen me to be the operator.

Of course, they told me that several people are looking at this prospect for the same amount of money to drill and that this would be subject to prior sale. It is my understanding that they gave a large sum for this acreage and they are now examining the title.

> If you are interested in this prospect with Texota, including OMNI Inc. or ENI Exploration Co., please get in touch with me by Tuesday, May 8, 1979, or sooner. I will be looking forward to hearing from you by telephone if you, OMNI or ENI are interested or not.
>
> Yours very truly,
> Olga Barrett

Once again Corpening Enterprises failed to reply to Olga's letter.

*****

Five months later, in October 1979, Texota Corporation drilled and completed the Faye Easley No. 1 well located on the Easley ranch across the fence from Corpening's Thompson No. 1 well. It was also a "gusher," flowing oil from the same conglomerate field as Corpening's Thompson No. 1 well. By that time, Easley had died and had left his wife, Faye Easley, as owner of the ranch and mineral interests. The record owner of the well was Texota Corporation and the official Texas state agency had granted Texota the right to drill the Easley well. There was no official deed record that evidenced the fact that Texota had been created for Olga Barrett. No official transfer had been recorded showing Olga Barrett to be the true owner of the oil lease.

The Corpenings, meanwhile, had watched from across the boundary fence without making any objection or filing any claim while Texota drilled and completed the Faye Easley No. 1 well on the northwest eighty acres of the southeast quarter of Section 23 at a place that Corpening Enterprises would have been entitled to buy under the original checkerboard agreement. Also, they had previously refused to give Olga Barrett any information to which she was entitled regarding the drilling, completion, and production of the Corpening's Thompson No. 1 well.

After Texota Corporation had drilled and completed and started producing the Faye Easley No. 1 well, the Corpening brothers, Scott and Joe Jr., then filed a civil suit in the Foard County courthouse in Crowell against Texota Corporation and Olga Barrett, claiming they were entitled to the well plus attorneys' fees. The suit was filed in August 1980, and Olga summoned Richard Bird and me for a meeting. I had hired Richard, a veteran local attorney, to assist me in the defense. We met in the district courtroom in the Quanah courthouse for a private conference. Olga was outraged, demanding not only a defense to the Corpening Enterprises lawsuit but also several cross-actions against Corpening. Richard and I knew that the cross-actions were without validity and would give them an open door to produce a lot of damaging testimony and documents that would spell disaster for our case. I told Olga her proposed plan would be disastrous to her defense, and I would not be a party to filing the actions. I told her that I would withdraw if she insisted on filing them.

Olga then looked at Richard Bird and said: "Well, Richard, you would stay with me, wouldn't you?"

Richard replied: "No, Olga, if Bill withdraws, then I will also."

Olga glared at us for a few minutes, then turned and walked across the courtroom and faced the corner. Everyone was silent for about ten minutes. Then Olga turned and came back to us and said: "Well, okay, I'm going to give y'all another chance."

We then settled down to discussing our strategy for the upcoming trial.

Richard and I agreed that to put Olga on the stand during the trial and subjecting her to cross-examination by opposing counsel would be disastrous. Our strategy for Olga was to keep her seated at the counsel table and keep her quiet. We did, in fact, then employ Richard's nephew, who had just graduated from law school, with the sole duty to sit beside Olga: "Keep her quiet! No outbursts!"

And we proceeded to trial.

We forced the Corpenings to admit that Olga had written to them two letters prior to Texota drilling the Faye Easley No. 1 well setting forth that Texota Corporation had secured an oil lease from Hartley Easley and had offered them an opportunity to participate in the drilling of a well on the Easley property just across the fence from their Thompson No. 1 well. The Corpenings sat back and took no action until after the well had been drilled and completed in October of 1979. The plaintiffs later called David Hooper to testify and forced him to admit that he had formed the Texota Corporation and he and his wife were the sole owners of the stock in that corporation. He also admitted that he had accompanied Franklin Coufal to see Hartley Easley and that Coufal, acting as a Texota agent, had succeeded in obtaining an oil and gas lease from him. The lease was signed March 14, 1979, and it covered his entire 960-acre ranch in Foard County, including the 160 acres where the Faye Easley No. 1 well was drilled. Hooper also admitted that Olga had paid him as her lawyer for the time he spent helping Franklin Coufal to obtain the lease and assigning it to the Texota Corporation. Further, he admitted that Olga Barrett had provided the funds that had been paid to Hartley Easley for obtaining the oil and gas lease on his property. At that time Hooper and his wife were not only the sole stockholders but also the official owners of Texota; and Texota Corporation was now the record owner of the Hartley Easley lease.

The map shows where the Corpening brothers had drilled the highly successful Thompson No. 1 well on one of their eighty-acre checkerboarded leases. Under her original agreement with Corpening, Olga had said that if she could get a lease on the Easley land, the Corpening brothers would be entitled to purchase from her one-half of it that included an eighty-acre tract in the southeast one-fourth of section 23. This did not come to pass.

By the time of the trial, Olga and David Hooper had become bitter enemies. Hooper felt he ought to have a large share of the Easley well, since he had done yeoman service in obtaining the Easley lease and assisted in filing all the documents required by the State of Texas in forming the Texota Corporation and in obtaining a permit from the state to drill the Easley well. But Olga viewed Hooper as her lawyer and not as her business partner. When Corpening's lawsuit went to trial, however, David Hooper, to his disgust, found himself not as Olga's lawyer in defending the lawsuit, but as a codefendant.

Richard Bird and I were employed to defend Olga at the trial resulting from the lawsuit. Hooper, on the other hand, had to defend himself.

Corpening Enterprises, of course, relied on their original agreement with Olga when they bought the checkerboarded eighty-acre tracts. That agreement stated that if Olga was able to obtain an oil and gas lease on the Easley tracts of land, she would include them in the checkerboarded lease grant to Corpening. But in Olga's defense, Richard Bird and I pointed out, and proved, that the Corpening agreement stated that if *Olga Barrett* later obtained an oil lease from Hartley Easley, then she would be obligated to include the Easley lands in the checkerboarded agreement with them. That was not the case. It was *Texota* that obtained a lease from Easley, which meant Olga was *not* required to transfer any of the Easley property to Corpening Enterprises. We also pointed out that Corpening had breached the original agreement by refusing to furnish Olga with drilling and completion records of their Thompson No. 1 well.

Later, during the trial, when David Hooper appeared to defend his interest, it was obvious that he was furious at Olga for forcing him to defend himself and could not avoid being saddled with a sizeable judgment against him that would amount to thousands of dollars. He had served as Olga's attorney during this entire episode and been paid only his hourly rate.

It also helped our cause that Richard Bird and I were hometown lawyers that had practiced often in the area small-town courts. Richard and I both lived within thirty miles of Crowell and often had appeared at the county and district courts of Foard County.

During the 1970s and early 1980s, few "big-city" lawyers ever had occasion to appear in our local courts. Consequently, none of the jurors or spectators had seen many big-shot lawyers from places like Dallas, Fort Worth, or that big city down the road of Abilene, Texas; especially a big-city lawyer like David Hooper, who wore white patent-leather shoes to court. Hooper's appearance did not help in his deposition or during cross-examination by Corpening's lawyers from Fort Worth. His extreme antagonism against Olga became very apparent as he attempted to blame her for his involvement.

Another advantage that helped my country-folk neighborly image in Foard County District Court was that I had attended the fifth and sixth grades in the Crowell Public School and personally knew several of the jurors.

During my closing argument to the jurors, when I needed to challenge David Hooper, I referred to those white shoes he was wearing as something inappropriate for any witness or attorney to wear when appearing before a rural jury. Several times when I wanted to challenge any testimony David Hooper had offered to the jury, I would preface my remarks to the jury by saying, "Now, Dr. White Shoes would have you believe…" and so forth. I underscored that remark to the jury by wearing my cowboy boots during the trial.

When all the trial testimony was finished and the jury was excused to retire to the jury room for deliberation on the fate of the contestants, one of the jurors I was well acquainted with looked back as they were departing and winked at me.

I knew then we had saved Aunt Olga's hide.

CHAPTER 26

Cosmetics, Oil Wells, and Cops
The Big Gawk

By the mid-1980s Texas was in the midst of an oil boom. It was said that you could stand at a deserted street corner in Dallas and whisper "oil" and draw a crowd instantly.

Everybody who was anybody, it seemed, was determined to get a piece of the action in the Texas oil patch. After Richard Bird and I rescued Aunt Olga in her Foard County court disputes with other oil producers, I was kept busy working from my Vernon law office representing clients—but even more occupied with oil patch matters, which included creating leases, drafting drilling contracts, researching land titles, and finding unleased acreage.

One of my new clients was Richard R. Rogers of Dallas, the wealthy son of the owner of Mary Kay Cosmetics—a company that still exists today and is doing quite well in the marketplace.

Son Richard decided that he would take time out of his life of leisure playing golf and partying with his millionaire friends to make yet another fortune, this time in the oil business. He organized the Triple R Exploration Company. "Triple R" was short for Richard R. Rogers. He set up the company headquarters in a luxurious second-floor office of the private Plano airport in North Dallas and hired me to acquire oil and gas leases in the Vernon area. I did purchase several oil leases in Hardeman, Wilbarger, and Foard Counties. And the company began drilling wells on those leases.

I kept my law office open in Vernon, but every couple of weeks I traveled to the Triple R headquarters in Plano to meet with the executives, geologists, and others. But Richard was never there. He had hired a friend to be the head of the company. We discussed open land acquisitions in the tri-county area, and I received instructions on where Triple R wanted to lease and where it planned seismic explorations, which led the geologists to recommend future drilling sites. Then I came back to the Vernon area, acquired leases, researched land titles, and prepared more drilling contracts.

One day in the mid-1980s, I was down in the plush Triple R offices in Plano discussing a drilling rig that Triple R had in the Hardeman County region when, all of a sudden, a flock of law enforcement officers broke into the office and announced they were investigating the Triple R Exploration Company, which they suspected of being a front for laundering illegal drug money. To say we all were stunned speechless by such allegations would be a great understatement!

As it later turned out, Triple R had hired two brothers from Weatherford—I'll call them Joe and Jim Jenkins for the purpose of this story. Joe and Jim were not connected with the geological matters of Triple R or lease and land acquisitions. The Jenkins brothers were only responsible for drilling the locations for Triple R wells. Joe and Jim were party boys and spent much time in Dallas clubs and golf courses and other places where attractive party girls were plentiful. At any rate, the law officers—mainly federal drug enforcement officers—believed that when the Jenkins brothers made their frequent flights from Plano to Mexico, they were buying drugs, taking them back to Dallas, and selling large quantities to their associates and shielding their sales proceeds from law enforcement by running the cash through the Triple R Exploration Company. This was a false premise and none of us at Triple R were involved or had even been aware that the Jenkins brothers were making frequent flights to Mexico to obtain narcotics.

All of us Triple R people were stunned when the drug enforcement officers began packing up all of our company records and carting them off to conduct their investigation.

Despite these shenanigans, none of the other Triple R employees were ever arrested or tried for any offense, including me. The Jenkins brothers were, however, arrested and put in jail immediately. They were found guilty of drug trafficking and sentenced to prison terms.

Fortunately, the drug enforcement officers had been recording not only telephone conversations between the Jenkins brothers but also conversations taking place in all of the Triple R offices, and none of us had made any incriminating comments.

That was a relief! Well, sort of a relief. It had the effect of throwing our oil business into quite a turmoil. Here the lawmen had packed up and removed all of the Triple R Exploration business records. This, mind you, was at a time when Triple R was drilling a well in Hardeman County and before records were regularly kept electronically. Result for us: we did not know who Triple R owed money to and who owed money to Triple R, nor what to do about that well that the Jenkins brothers had been drilling. After the dust cleared and all the lawmen had departed with our company records, we were in one hell of a mess!

To my amazement, the Triple R officials named me to take over as general manager of the company. Immediately. My first duty was to find somebody in the oil patch fraternity to take over as boss of the drilling rig, and then to track down all those accounts payable and receivable. The good part was that Triple R agreed to pay me a salary of $10,000 a month. (In 2018 dollars, $10,000 would be equal to $23,411.59.)

RRR EXPLORATION, INC.

BILL NEAL
GENERAL MANAGER

4300 WESTGROVE
DALLAS, TEXAS 75248
(214) 931-2403

VERNON, TEXAS
TELEPHONE
(817) 553-3391

Triple R Exploration, Inc. business card
of general manager, Bill Neal.

To make a very long story short, I did manage to hire a drilling expert to take over the drilling of the well in Hardeman County. And after many phone calls and conversations with various companies, we were finally able to get the financial side of Triple R back on track. Although that first well turned out to be a dry hole, we did drill several more wells and achieved great success in hitting oil.

Standing on the drilling platform of the Triple R Exploration drill site on Bowcher lease about two miles west of Chillicothe in Hardeman County, Texas. On left, Willie Rey, driller and on the right, Bill Neal, general manager of Triple R Exploration, circa 1982.

*****

You know, I've really enjoyed sitting here in my easy chair in my den, legs propped up, spinning this yarn. Especially the day us oil patch guys were sitting in that fancy Dallas office discussing where to drill the next well, when, without a knock, here a swarm of cops burst in the door, and with no explanation—nary a word—disappeared with all of our office business records.

None of us had spoken either. Just sat there in stunned silence. Thinking, surely this is a nightmare. Surely, we'll wake up in a minute and get out of bed. Then followed one of the longest, quietest gawks I've ever endured. Eyes wide, like somebody just goosed us in the ass, our mouths wide open, looking back and forth expecting somebody to explain…something.

At last the big gawk ended.

Somebody finally muttered: "What the hell was that all about?"

It seems really funny now that I'm leaning back in my easy chair sipping a frosty.

CHAPTER 27

Ropin' a Goat—Almost

In 1992 I decided to run for district attorney, this time in the Fiftieth Judicial District of Texas, not too far from where I lived on my Warriors Hollow Ranch.

One evening after I had wrapped up a hard day of campaigning and was leaving Paducah heading for home, I noticed an older couple attempting to load some goats into a trailer. The goats had been enclosed in a large backyard that included several acres. The enclosure was cluttered with several abandoned plows, old tractors, and other farm implements where the couple was chasing the goats in an attempt to load them into the trailer. I thought that I would stop and help load the goats.

I went into the large backyard and introduced myself and told the old lady that I was running for DA of that four-county area and that I would be glad to help them load the goats into the trailer. Together we renewed the chase. This went on for quite a spell and we finally had all the goats loaded, except for one. He was a wily old billy goat and he kept eluding capture. I told the woman that I would try to rope that goat. She produced a rope and gave it to me. But I was unable to get within roping range.

Finally, she said, "Well, we've got a motorcycle. Maybe you could use that to get close enough to rope the goat."

I replied, "Lady, I can rope and I can ride a motorcycle, but I can't ride a motorcycle and rope a goat at the same time."

She stopped, looked at me, and with hands on her hips said, "Well, what the hell kind of district attorney would you make anyway?"

Without a word or reply, I shrugged my shoulders, turned, and walked away.

I bet they hadn't registered to vote anyhow.

CHAPTER 28

Maintaining Law and Order in "the Big Empty" Sheriff Jim Waller in Charge

The small town of Guthrie is the county seat of King County and is located in the heart of the Big Empty. Let me pause here to describe what us West Texans call "the Big Empty." Located about seventy miles south of the southeastern corner of the Texas panhandle is a town called Benjamin. It marks the beginning of a distinctly different kind of ranch country—a huge and remote chunk of northwest Texas so sparsely populated that it would seem no self-respecting animal could ever make its home there. It is a dry and windswept land of rough cedar breaks, steep canyons, buttes, mesas, a few cottonwood and hackberry trees in dry draws, and some mesquite-dotted grassy flats. This broken prairie land rolls on westward from Benjamin before it runs headlong into the rearing Caprock escarpment defining the eastern edge of the Staked Plains of far West Texas and the Texas panhandle.

Wild things live there—small creatures mostly, such as coyotes and jackrabbits and rattlesnakes—as well as some cattle and still fewer human beings. It is a lonely, yet hauntingly beautiful country, so vast and sweeping that it dwarfs mere men and horses and cattle, somehow conveying the sense that it is a land that time has passed by, that lies patiently awaiting the return of great prehistoric beasts—inhabitants more fitting to the hushed vastness.

Lone cowboy viewing the sprawling "Big Empty," which includes King County, Texas, drawn by Jimmy Clay in 2018.

*****

I had just been elected district attorney of the Fiftieth Judicial District. It was a heated race, but I won and was elected. I won a majority vote in three of the four counties. I didn't win a majority of the vote in King County—but neither did my opponent. We ended up in a deadlock: eighty-seven votes for my opponent and eighty-seven votes for me. Goes to show why King County was called "the heart of the Big Empty." The tiny village of Guthrie is the biggest town in King County. In fact, it was, and still is, the only town in the county.

The borders of King County form a square—thirty miles east to west and thirty miles north to south—and only one small highway, State Highway 83, cuts the county in half. Guthrie, at the time, had only three buildings: a combination service station and café, a school, and a courthouse in which was located the King County sheriff's office when I took over as DA in 1992.

And that office was the headquarters of King County Sheriff Jim Waller. Sheriff Waller had no deputies—and really, he needed none. During the twelve years I served as DA in that district, only one major crime was committed in King County.

Nevertheless, to say that Sheriff Waller took his position as the chief—and only—law enforcement officer of King County seriously would be a gross understatement. Each and every day, Sheriff Waller was out and about roaming all over King County diligently ensuring that all the residents could go about their lives and business in peace.

As district attorney I usually made the rounds of each of the four district courts at least once a month, even if there were no criminal trials scheduled in the courts. Whenever my investigator Chuck Morris and I stopped off at the King County courthouse, Sheriff Waller always made it a point to be there to confer with us. He would greet us, usher us into his office, close the door behind us to ensure privacy and confidentiality, then brief us on his ongoing efforts to keep the peace in King County. On several occasions Sheriff Waller even assured us that he had contacts with the KBI (the Kansas Bureau of Investigation), and once even mentioned that he had a special contact inside Interpol (the International Police Organization located in Paris, France).

My investigator and I both kept notes on Sheriff Waller's adventures—even the part about his alleged contacts with the KBI and Interpol—with rapt attention, never once even cracking a smile. However, when we got back in our car and departed, Chuck's dry sense of humor would come to the surface. Chuck commented, "You know, we're sure lucky to have an important lawman contact with Interpol out here in King County. Sheriff Waller says he reports almost daily to Interpol. Can't you just hear Interpol's office people over there in France if Sheriff Waller failed to call in his daily report? I bet one of the chief investigators sits back with great anticipation just waiting for the sheriff's call every morning. Can't you hear him say every morning: 'It's ten o'clock and Sheriff Waller hasn't called in yet.' He waits another ten minutes. Still no call. Walks to the chief's office and says, 'Chief, it's ten minutes after ten and we still haven't heard a word from Sheriff Waller over in Guthrie, Texas. I'm real concerned. Think we ought to dispatch one of our New York contacts to send up an immediate alarm. Sheriff Waller's never been this late calling in his report!'"

*****

On all subsequent stopovers at Sheriff Waller's office, the sheriff would assure us that he was relentlessly keeping the peace in King County and always on the lookout for lawbreakers. One time he informed us that he had recently spent hours hidden on top of a small ridge that overlooked the only liquor store in King County, located about ten miles east of Guthrie. His mission was to ensure that the owner was not surreptitiously selling any liquor to minors or dealing in any bootleg whiskey. Not that the liquor store owner had ever been convicted, or even charged, with any criminal offense. In fact, that liquor store owner happened to also be a King County commissioner. Still, Sheriff Waller assured us that he could not be too careful in discharging his law enforcement duties.

All in all, the residents of King County were satisfied with their sheriff. I did, however, receive one complaint about Sheriff Waller's overzealous enforcement of his duties as a dedicated law enforcement official. The call came from the owner of a trucking firm who owned several oil tanker trucks that traveled some of the King County dirt roads to load oil from oil well storage tanks and haul it back to town. Once, after a soaking rain, one of their trucks carrying a heavy load had made deep ruts in the mud. A King County farmer complained to Sheriff Waller that the deep ruts the oil tanker had left caused him difficulty driving to town. Sheriff Waller certainly took the complaint seriously. He issued a ticket to the oil company for "ruttin' the roads"—a criminal offense that was not mentioned in any Texas law book.

*****

Nevertheless, Sheriff Waller was ever alert for villains and always on guard against potential vicious criminals. At some point he attended a law enforcement get-together during which someone lectured on the rise of a sect of devil worshippers who represented a serious threat to the lives and properties of law-abiding Christian citizens. Sheriff Waller, when he returned home, decided to undertake a serious investigation to thwart any such devil worshippers who might be lurking anywhere in King County.

He had been informed that devil worshippers often left signs and symbols on their secret meeting places. Therefore, Sheriff Waller began inspecting all buildings in downtown Guthrie as well as all the small family barns and outhouses for those devil worshippers' signs and symbols. After one such mission, Sheriff Waller returned to his office to find a message from a farmer's wife who had noticed some fellow creeping around their barn. Concerned about potential threats to their safety and property, she had called the sheriff's office to report this skulking intruder. Sheriff Waller, after receiving the message, was forced to call the next day and assure the poor lady that it was he who she had seen. He had merely been making the rounds of all buildings that might be harboring those dangerous devil worshippers.

*****

As I said, there was really only one very serious crime committed in King County during Sheriff Waller's tenure in office. One night, a couple of college kids who lived in the eastern edge of the Texas panhandle in the little town of Shamrock were killed on State Highway 83 while traveling back to college. Another young man was driving the opposite direction on SH 83 when he pulled out to pass a truck and ran head on into the college kids' car, killing both of them. The driver of the other car, the young man who pulled out into the left lane to pass the truck, was apparently very intoxicated. He was indicted for manslaughter by a King County grand jury.

Sheriff Waller, therefore, anticipated that a sensational jury trial would be scheduled in the county in the near future, and that he, the reigning law enforcement officer in the county, would have a very important duty to perform in assisting the court during the trial. If so, then a large number of people would attend the trial. Since there were no hotels, cafés, or other accommodations in King County, he knew there would be a problem in taking care of the crowd of witnesses for both the prosecution and the defense, potential jurors, as well as a large number of spectators. The sheriff realized that during the trial he would be the gatekeeper in addition to being in charge of all arrangements.

Sheriff Waller decided that if and when a jury trial took place, he would not be found guilty of failing to take proper care of all these arrangements. He would be "the man in charge." He even arranged to have two prefabricated structures hauled to Guthrie and placed on the courthouse square, and food service available for the crowds.

What Sheriff Waller did not anticipate was what actually happened. Prior to the anticipated jury trial, the prosecuting attorney and the defense attorney arrived at a plea bargain agreement. Hence, no jury trial ever occurred, much to Sheriff Jim Waller's disappointment.

I was told that the King County officials were more than a little disgruntled when they received all the statements detailing the expenses that Sheriff Waller had incurred during his painstaking efforts in setting up for the courtroom battle of the century—the one that never happened.

*****

Sheriff Waller would later have a starring role in another King County crime drama that didn't quite turn out as expected. (This one also put an unexpected dent in King County's budget.)

One night, Sheriff Waller decided to patrol lonely SH 83 to snare any outlaws that might be up to some illegal shenanigans. He was alone driving the King County sheriff's car when he got into a gun battle with some suspicious characters driving in another vehicle. Exactly why Sheriff Waller stopped the suspects wasn't clear. In his report, he said that he had stopped that suspicious vehicle several miles south of Guthrie, adding that one or more of the outlaws then opened fire on him, and he returned the fire. Luckily, the sheriff was not wounded. According to his report, the outlaws got back in their car and drove away. Sheriff Waller could not provide a description of the car, the license plate number of the car, or the number of outlaws who had fired at him. However, Sheriff Waller's car did have several bullet holes in it when he drove it back to Guthrie later that night.

The next morning, he got around to alerting officers in the surrounding area about the gun battle. The suspects were never identified or found, and nobody admitted to participating in the gun battle. Nobody was ever arrested. But Sheriff Waller continued to brag about his heroic shootout with those desperadoes.

Other lawmen, the following day, came up with some troubling questions that were never answered. Number one, why hadn't Sheriff Waller immediately notified someone—especially other area lawmen? Why did the sheriff wait until the next morning to report the incident? And how come he had a number of bullet holes in his sheriff's car, but none had hit him? And also, upon reflection, how come none of those bullets had penetrated any vital car parts such as his radiator, disabling his vehicle and preventing him from driving back to Guthrie?

But the real clincher came the next day when the sheriff of Stonewall County, the county adjoining King County to the south, filed his report. It turned out that by pure chance, the Stonewall County sheriff had been out patrolling SH 83 that same night and had parked on a ridge immediately south of the King County line at the same time Sheriff Waller reported that the shooting had taken place. If the outlaws had fled in their vehicle heading south on SH 83, he would have seen them pass by. But the Stonewall County sheriff reported that no vehicle had come past him on the highway heading south (or even heading north) at any time that night.

The next month, King County commissioners received a hefty repair bill for rehabilitating Sheriff Waller's bullet-riddled vehicle.

The brave King County sheriff did not seek reelection when his term expired. The last I heard of ex-sheriff Jim Waller, he had departed the county and headed south to the town of Kerrville, I think, and was engaged in the business of selling used cars.

CHAPTER 29

The Saga of Bob More
How Monopoly Money Resolved a Courtroom Battle between Two Brothers

One day while I was sitting in my law office in Vernon, Texas, across the street from the Wilbarger County courthouse, a man named Bob More walked in and said that he wanted to hire me to represent him in an estate matter. His mother, Gladys Cronin "Ann Christy" More, had died the previous year in November. As it turned out, Ann Christy had been a movie actress and had acted during the 1920s and 1930s. She appeared in several movies, including one movie with Bing Crosby in 1931 titled *Dream House*. In 1932, Ann Christy costarred with Edward J. Nugent in her last movie titled *Behind Stone Walls*. But her acting career came to an end when she married Robert L. More Jr. on August 3 later that same year in Vernon, Texas. In fact, she was still residing in Vernon on the date of her death.

Robert Jr. and Ann Christy became acquainted and fell in love while he was attending the University of California in Los Angeles. At that time, he was friends with Jimmy Stewart and some other Hollywood celebrities.

Soon they had two sons: Robert L. "Bob" More III, born in September of 1934; and, nine years later, Patrick Christy "Pat" More. Initially, I didn't believe that my task as lawyer for Bob More would be very difficult or complicated. After all, Mrs. More's will had been admitted to probate without contest and there were no pending lawsuits involving the estate. The only problem seemed to be dividing the estate properties equally between the two heirs, Bob and his younger brother, Pat. Although Pat had been named executor of Mrs. More's estate, Bob and Pat could not agree how to divide the properties they co-owned between themselves.

Bob had employed me to represent him, and Pat had hired Richard Bird, a respected attorney from Childress and also a good friend of mine. But my initial conclusion that dividing the More estate between the two brothers would be a rather simple matter to resolve turned out to be a gross miscalculation on my part.

Let me pause here and give you some background of this story. Bob and Pat's grandfather, Robert L More Sr., was employed for many years as the estate manager of the Waggoner empire, which had a large office building in downtown Vernon where his office was located. The Waggoner empire included a 520,000-acre ranch covering approximately eight hundred square miles, the largest under one fence in the United States at that time. It stretched into six counties with its main ranching headquarters, Zacaweista, located thirteen miles south of Vernon.

During his career, Robert L. More Sr. also established his own wholesale and retail gasoline business, opened the first movie house in Vernon, and acquired a lot of real estate. His son Robert L. More Jr. worked as a junior partner in his father's oil business and later established the Robert L. More Tire Company in Vernon. Robert L. More Jr. died in 1972, leaving his entire estate to his wife, Ann Christy More.

Although under the terms of their mother's will the brothers were co-owners of these properties, they could not agree which brother got sole ownership of which property, and they were not willing to continue owning all these properties jointly. The brothers did not like each other, and their personalities were as different as bourbon and buttermilk. Both brothers were very intelligent, but that is where their similarities ended.

Bob and his wife, Mercedes ("Mercy"), lived in northeastern New Mexico on the historic Phoenix Ranch, which had been a gift to Bob on his first birthday from his grandfather, Robert L. More

Sr. The Phoenix ranch had originally been owned by a western pioneer, Sam Watrous, and was located about five miles from the town of Watrous, New Mexico. The Phoenix ranch sits in a lush valley between the Great Plains to the east and the foothills of the Rockies to the west and is an equal distance of approximately eighty miles from Taos, Santa Fe, and Raton, New Mexico. The main residence is a large territorial-style house built in 1862 during the Civil War.

Robert L More Sr. purchased the Phoenix Ranch located at the crossing of the old Santa Fe Trail and the Mora River in the northeastern part of New Mexico near the town of Watrous. He offered it to WT Waggoner, but Waggoner declined the offer saying it was too small and too far away from the Waggoner Ranch in Texas. Robert L More Sr. gave the Phoenix Ranch to his grandson, Robert L "Bob" More III as a gift on his first birthday. The ranch headquarters was a 5,000 square foot Territorial style house that was built in 1862.

Bob was very gregarious as well as a very talented artisan. He had his own shop on the ranch, where he designed and made different kinds of guns, and a studio, where he created one-of-a-kind pieces of jewelry. Bob enjoyed making the guns for himself and the pieces of jewelry as gifts for his wife.

When Bob and Mercy became acquainted, she had recently graduated from Midwestern University in Wichita Falls and was employed as a junior high math teacher in Vernon. At the end of her first year of teaching, the superintendent called her into his office and gave her this ultimatum. "Miss Rizo, you can either teach here for another year or you can date Bobby More, but you're not going to do both." Mercy did continue to date and eventually marry Bob, which ended her teaching career.

On one of their first dates, Mercy asked Bob how he made his living. He said, "Let's go on a two-week fishing trip to my ranch in New Mexico, and when we return to Vernon I will get a job." They did go to the Phoenix ranch for two weeks, but they never did return to Vernon, except briefly to get married, and then made their home on the Phoenix ranch.

In 1956 Robert L "Bob" More III married Mercedes "Mercy" Rizo pictured above. Mercy was a math teacher at Vernon Intermediate School at that time. The happy couple made their home on the Phoenix Ranch near Watrous, New Mexico.

Pat and his wife, Diane, lived in Vernon. Diane had three daughters when they married and soon there was a son and another daughter. Diane was also an accomplished musician and had played with the Dallas Symphony. From time to time, Diane would go back to Dallas and play concerts with the symphony.

To describe Pat as a penny-pinching tightwad would not be an overstatement of his character. After the properties had been divided between the two brothers, Pat and his family moved into the Robert L. More Sr. family home on the outskirts of Vernon. The home was a mansion with more than one floor and even included a beautiful upstairs ballroom for entertaining. However, Pat partitioned off only five or six rooms of the mansion for his family to use in order to save money on the cost of maintenance and utilities. To save money on food, Pat once purchased large cases of canned hominy, which was the basic family diet for quite a spell. While the children were young, Pat and his wife were once prompted from one of the local schoolteachers to buy the children proper winter clothing. It was rumored that once when Pat and Diane went to Dallas for Diane to play in a musical program performed by the Dallas Symphony, they didn't bother to stay in a motel overnight. They avoided that expense by parking their automobile in a friend's driveway and spending the night in the car.

Pat was always, however, a thrifty and successful businessman; and over the years he accumulated a large estate and today is active in preserving the history of the Vernon community through his work with the Red River Valley Museum.

*****

But getting back to the problem for which the brothers hired Richard Bird and me. Let's state it this way: the brothers did not want to continue to own the properties jointly. Each brother desired to have total ownership of certain individual properties in the estate. After several months of working on a solution and a number of court appearances, the estate problem was still unresolved. It was clear to Richard and me that to arrive at a practical solution, we had to place a monetary value for each property. This we agreed to resolve by assigning to each property the current ad valorem tax value that had been placed by the county officials. But we were still stuck with the problem of not only who got first choice of which property but how to devise a plan so that each brother ended up with the same monetary value of the divided properties. Richard and I finally concocted a novel plan.

This is the plan we adopted. We added up the total value of all of the properties, went to the local dime store and bought a large number of Monopoly games, and counted out enough Monopoly game money to total the amount of the properties to be divided. Then we gave each brother an equal share of the Monopoly money. At that point, we flipped a coin to see which brother got first choice of the property that he wanted to buy. That brother had to pay for it out of his share of the Monopoly money, which either Richard or I collected. Then the other brother took his turn and made his purchase for a property. And so it went until all of the money was spent and all properties were purchased. At long last the estate was divided equally between Bob and Pat. Richard Bird and I prepared deeds for the brothers to execute and make ownership of the properties official. And that is how each brother became sole owner of his half of their mother's estate.

*****

My relationship with Bob More, whether representing him as a client or in our personal friendship, has always produced some unexpected results. For instance, once when seated in the courtroom in Vernon, I noticed that Bob had brought in a very large Bible and had set it on our table. I was very puzzled by the appearance of this Bible, as I had not known Bob to be a particularly religious person. I looked at him and remarked, "What the hell is this Bible doing in here?" Bob looked at me with a sheepish grin and without a word opened the Bible. Much to my amazement an inner portion of the Bible pages had been cut out, and ensconced inside lay a pistol. He just grinned at me and shrugged. I said, "Get that damn thing out of this courtroom and take it to my office and leave it there!"

After we had concluded the courtroom battle for ownership of estate properties, my wife and I, at Bob and Mercy's invitation, spent some time visiting them at their Phoenix ranch in New Mexico. Again, there were some very interesting and unexpected incidences. Once, while my wife and I were visiting with Bob and Mercy in their kitchen, Bob unexpectedly reached into his pants pocket and pulled out a revolver with the hammer already cocked. I was astounded. So, I said, "Oh, did you make that pistol?" He nodded his head and I said, "Let me see it." He handed me the pistol, I feigned great interest in his workmanship, looked it over carefully, and slowly let the hammer back to ensure the pistol would not be fired accidentally. I complimented his workmanship and then handed the pistol back to him. Much to my amazement, Bob cocked the pistol once again and stuck it back into his pants pocket.

In a later conversation with Mercy, she mentioned to me that Bob would often put on his cowboy outfit, strap on his holster containing his pistol, and go to town to show off his workmanship. But one day Mercy received a call asking her to stop bringing Bob to town wearing his pistol. Turns out it was making some of the local residence very uncomfortable.

Bob had an interest not only in guns but also in dynamite and blowing up things. One day when Bob was outside their home shooting at dynamite that he had tied to the top of a post, he noticed his friend, a state policeman named Bob Richie, driving toward the house. In anticipation of his stopping to visit, Bob More put a bucket over the dynamite. When Bob Richie got out of the car, he asked his friend what he was doing and Bob answered, "Just doing a little target practice." The trooper asked if he could practice with him and Bob said, "Sure." That's when the trooper took out his pistol and shot at the target, which was the bucket. The dynamite exploded and knocked that trooper right on his rump. Needless to say, that ended target practice for the day.

When we visited with Bob and Mercy in New Mexico we could always anticipate another very interesting episode in the saga of Bob More. Fortunately, however, there was no more courthouse battles.

CHAPTER 30

Coming Back Home
Retirement on the Hackberry Ranch

Shortly after retiring, I learned that Diane Drake Waldo owned a place about ten miles southeast of Quanah which was for sale. I bought it and named it the Hackberry Ranch. I was familiar with the land, a tranquil and serene place with numerous varieties of wildlife and no public roads nearby with noisy traffic. Indeed, it is a beautiful ranch that has a very sentimental appeal to me for several reasons. Its southern boundary is the north boundary of what was the Medicine Mound Ranch that I grew up on, and looking to the east you can see the four mounds that are located on the old Neal Ranch. On the other side of those mounds is the little village of Medicine Mound, where I attended first grade. To me being there felt like I was coming back home.

Entrance gate to our Hackberry Ranch.

Aerial photo of the home of Bill and Gayla Neal on the Hackberry Ranch. It is positioned on a peninsula located between two lakes. The ranch is located some four miles west of the little village of Medicine Mound and approximately fifteen miles south of Quanah, Texas.

In 1997, a very attractive, intelligent. and loving woman named Gayla Ulrich and I fell in love and got married. We both have children from prior marriages. Gayla has two daughters and I have two sons and one daughter. All these children are adults and living their separate lives. We also have one very special four-year-old grandson, Magnus.

When Gayla and I decided to erect a home, I wanted to be sure no one could sell it out from under us or disrupt the peacefulness. That is why I decided to buy the ranch. It would be a perfect place for us to enjoy and realize our vision to enhance its beauty and serenity.

We began by taking advantage of an area where two draws come together and create a watershed. We had two ponds dug there with a strip of land in between and stocked them with fish. That strip of land, when cleared of brush with its hackberry and other trees, became the perfect spot to build a vacation home. It became a place where family and friends could come for a visit or a retreat for Gayla and me to enjoy together.

Aerial photo of Hackberry Ranch with
mounds in the background.

Texas historians, Bill O'Neal (apostrophe) and Bill O. Neal (period) at the Hackberry Ranch entrance near Quanah, Texas. Nicknames are a result of both names having an "O" in the middle. When visiting they endearingly address each other by their designated nickname.

Bill O'Neal was appointed the third Texas State Historian by Governor Rick Perry. He held that post for six years from 2012 to September 2018. That was only a brief part of Bill's long career as a western frontier historian. He was a professor at Panola College in Carthage, Texas for many years and has written over fifty nonfiction books and still writing. I was honored by Bill recently when he dedicated his book, *John Chisum, Frontier Cattle King* published by Eakin Press in 2018 to me.

Upon completion of our home, we furnished it with family furniture pieces from earlier years as well as artwork and memorabilia that provide a casual stroll through the good times of our past. Best of all, the view is not cluttered with any other nearby homes or buildings. In the fall we are treated to the annual migration of ducks and geese arriving and alighting on the ponds. There are also many other species of birds, such as quail, dove, and wild turkey. as well as deer. Almost daily one can see fish jumping from the surface of the ponds, and that often encourages one or both of us to mosey down to the pond for a spell of fishing. Horses have also been a welcomed addition to the ranch for many years.

Horses have been a welcomed addition to the ranch for many years. Pictured (left to right) Chamaco, Tuffy Shane, and Rusty.

Also, views from the observation tower inspire fond memories of the past. Looking at the four mounds brings back several memories of the village of Medicine Mound where I spent the first four years of my schooling before the Medicine Mound school was consolidated with the Quanah school district.

Fred Simmons was and is not only a close personal friend but was and is almost like a brother. I have known him almost my whole life. Fred is a multitalented person, especially when it comes to engineering projects. A few years before purchasing the Hackberry Ranch, I bought a portion of the abandoned railroad right-of-way of the Kansas City Mexico and Orient railroad. We have used much of the gravel to improve ranch roads and the railroad ties from the tracks to build a barn and fencing. One day Fred suggested that we use the huge twenty-eight-foot timbers from the Pease River railroad bridge to construct an observation tower. I agreed, and he designed and built it near our ranch home. The tower provides wonderful views of the ranch and surrounding area. Fred also designed and engineered the ponds project. He dug both of them and built the dams.

Old friends, Fred Simmons and Bill Neal visiting in the backyard of the ranch home. Fred Simmons, a friend who has lived all his life in the nearby area, has often been employed by the author to perform or oversee all kinds of ranch jobs. He operates heavy machinery on the ranch including tractors, plows, caterpillars, and other large equipment, even inventing some when necessary. He dug both lakes and constructed the dams that are located on the ranch. Fred's father, Street Simmons, now deceased, worked for the Neal family for many years to do similar work.

The tower stands a few yards from the Hackberry Ranch home and is thirty feet tall. It provides a wonderful view of the surrounding area including the Medicine Mounds to the east.

*****

Some years ago, my fascination with criminal law and my experience as a criminal lawyer led me to begin collecting and researching old tales of criminal trials—murder cases in particular. I started a serious pursuit that had always intrigued me: researching the post-Civil War history of West Texas, the Oklahoma Territory, and eastern New Mexico. I became convinced that many of these yarns were just too good to be left buried and forgotten. Fortunately, Gayla was also interested in writing and reading books, especially nonfiction books containing tales of history. So Gayla and I began spending many hours digging into those old stories, rummaging through musty records in courthouse basements, and sifting through the dusty morgues of local weekly newspapers. County history books became an obsession. Occasionally, we would find a local historian who helped fill in the gaps. Once in a while we were even able to interview people with personal knowledge of the events.

We discovered that in almost all of these tales of early-day murders and murder trials, the accused, either by jury verdict or by some legal high jinks, managed to be found not guilty. Why, we continued to wonder, and by what means? The stories themselves go a long way toward answering these questions, but a fuller understanding depends on an appreciation of the time, place, and culture in which they occurred. It was a time before prosecution of criminal cases was aided by fingerprints, DNA, and other scientific methods of verifying incriminating evidence. Both of us subscribe to the idea that nonfiction books should be an enjoyable read for anyone interested in history.

This research has resulted in six nonfiction books published by university presses—four by Texas Tech University Press and two by North Texas University Press. The modicum of fame and fortune I received from these books sent me across the state and the region to deliver speeches and sign copies for fans. It has been a rewarding endeavor to fill my retirement years.

Book Signing at the public library in Vernon, Texas Seated are Steve Brantley and Bill Neal, December 9, 2015.

Gayla and I continue to enjoy the Hackberry Place as well as researching and writing nonfiction stories that reflects the statement, "Truth is often stranger than fiction."

Bill and Gayla Neal in the Hackberry Ranch home.

CHAPTER 31

Returning to Austin

Returning to Austin in May 2019 was truly a highlight of the year for me. I attended a reunion with my classmates of the University of Texas Law School class of 1964. It was our first-class reunion in fifty-five years! Great fun and storytelling filled the days and evenings.

1964 University of Texas Law School graduates in attendance at the 55th Class Reunion. Standing (left to right) Lynn Coleman, Irwin Steinhorn, Bill Neal, Ken Glaser, and Shannon Ratliff. Lynn R. Coleman retired from a Washington D.C. law firm, Skadden, Arps, Slate, Meagher & Flom LLP & Affiliates in 2003. He specialized in energy regulation and litigation. Irwin Steinhorn is currently a lawyer specializing in corporate, securities, and environmental law with Conner & Winters LLP in Oklahoma City, Oklahoma. William O. "Bill" Neal is a retired criminal lawyer. He served as a prosecutor in two different Texas Judicial Districts for a total of twenty years. He also had a private general practice for many years. Kenneth "Ken" R. Glaser is an international intellectual property lawyer with Foley & Lardner LLP in Dallas, Texas. Shannon H. Ratliff is a trial and appellate lawyer that specializes in oil and gas litigation with Davis, Gerald & Cremer, a professional corporation in Austin, Texas.

EPILOGUE

Recently, I was interviewed by Kay Ellington and Barbara Brannon, co-creators of Lone Star Literary Life, a website that provides weekly information for readers, writers, booksellers, librarians and authors (which can be found at www.lonestarliterary.com). I felt like my interview might be of interest to those individuals interested in reading or writing about western history.

The following is that interview:

*****

Texas attorney and author Bill Neal knows the law—and he knows how to spin a tale. He has combined his skill in observation of fact with a keen knowledge of Texas history and an ear for the telling detail, to publish some of the most fascinating accounts of frontier law and life in print. When you ask Bill a question, you'd better sit down for the answer, because he'll take the long way around. But it'll sure be worth the trip.

Congratulations on the publication of yet another rousing book about Texas justice. You're an attorney and an author. How do the two professions complement each other?

During the thirty-nine years I practiced law in small West Texas counties I learned much, not only about criminal law practice, but also about many events that had occurred in the vast area of West Texas that had never received much attention in newspapers, television, or books. Many were criminal cases that had never been solved, or even if so, there was much more to the cases that hadn't been printed or covered by the media. I began to see that there were many more fascinating true stories that could be told and which included facts and twists that had never been revealed to the public. I began researching and writing.

What was your first big break as an author?

Several years before I retired from active law practice, I began writing drafts of various tales that begged to be told. I had no instructions on writing or marketing such books. I just sat down and started telling a story, but I soon realized that they needed considerable "polishing up" before submitting them to any university press.

One day—I believe in 2002—when I was a prosecutor for the 50th Judicial District, which included the little town of Benjamin in Knox County, State Photographer of Texas Wyman Meinzer came to my office and wanted help with a copyright infringement matter. He and I became friends, and I told him of my ambition to find a university publisher for my stories. Wyman was well acquainted with Judith Keeling, editor of Texas Tech University Press, and put me in touch with her. She saw my drafts, helped me select and arrange the material, and published my first book.

Once with the submission of another manuscript to a university press editor, I ran into an apparent roadblock. The editor, before accepting my manuscript, had to follow its standard procedure of submitting a proposed manuscript to three anonymous experts for approval. Two of those voted thumbs-up on my manuscript. But the third refused at first, saying that while my story was very interesting and would appeal to many readers, my "informal" writing style was "beneath the dignity of a university press."

I aimed to tell a documented nonfiction western story, but it was not submitted as a scholarly treatise or thesis. And I cited a quote from noted historian and best-selling author David McCullough: "No harm is done to history by making it something that someone would want to read." I went on to say that I attempted to be a good and documented storyteller and avoided long boring sentences burdened by scholarly jargon or by the legalese of an appellate court brief. Finally, I won approval of the editor.

Your books deal with Western history and law and order. Did you read a lot of Western titles growing up? What kinds of books/authors did you enjoy reading?

Mark Twain was—and is—my favorite author. I also like the fiction stories of Elmore Leonard, several of which are the basis for some Hollywood films. And Civil War stories, biographies, and autobiographies of famous people, outlaws and lawmen as well as others, have always fascinated me.

I like Western nonfiction authors such as Sallie Reynolds Matthews, Frederick Nolan, Leon Metz, Bill O'Neal, Chuck Parsons, J. Evetts Haley, Walter Prescott Webb, J. Frank Dobie, Glenn Shirley, John Miller Morris, and others.

You've turned out a lot of books in recent years. What's your creative process like?

My creative process is usually kicked off when I discover a tale with great potential—one that has never received much publicity. As pointed out above, I practiced law for thirty-nine years, and during that time my practice took me to many small towns in West Texas. Frequently, I came across stories—sometimes fragmented stories of lawmen and outlaws, of crimes and trials, etc., and I would think: *You know, there has to be a lot more to this story than this little tidbit.* My curiosity would be piqued. I couldn't stop mulling it over in my mind, so I would begin my research down that cold trail.

What advice would you give to aspiring authors?

This advice is for writers of nonfiction books, or for novels based on real incidents. The advice is this: research, research, research. Then write a draft. Then research, research, and research. Then rewrite, rewrite, rewrite. Then maybe even more research.

Researching can become addictive, and you will probably feel that part of the work is never going to end. I have often started down the researching trail of some historical quest, but that trail almost always has a trail with many forks in the road. It often raises more questions than answers. So you can spend forever searching down those dusty side trails of the past.

I know one devoted Western history buff who has been chasing rabbits down all those old trails for years but has never actually written a book. Sometimes you just have to go with what you have. My experience as a newspaper reporter taught me that at some point in time, you just "gotta let go and go with what you got." One time, I discovered a very important fact several years after I had concluded a story in a previous book. It was so important that I used it as the basis for a subsequent book.

9.24.2017 Abilene author Bill Neal on journalism, mentors, and "making history something someone would want to read"

Interview picture of Bill Neal as it appeared
on the Lone Star Literary Life website,
www.lonestarliterary.com September 24, 2017.

৩৩

ACKNOWLEDGMENTS

Many thanks are in order to those who have assisted me in writing this book of stories. To my former law partner and close friend, Paul Scott of Sweetwater, Texas; and to another close friend of many moons, the official Texas State Historian, Bill O'Neal of Carthage, Texas. Bill has written many exhaustively researched books of history, not only of Texas but also of the Western frontier. When Bill O'Neal and I see each other or talk on the phone, I refer to him as "Apostrophe," and he calls me "Period," because my middle name begins with an O. He is Bill O'Neal and I am Bill O. Neal. Recently, Bill honored me by dedicating to me his book *John Chism: Frontier Cattle King*, a biography of a New Mexico frontier cattleman published in 2018.

I also need to acknowledge Chuck Morris of Seymour, Texas, my former criminal investigator who served with me while I was the district attorney in a multicounty rural area. Chuck provided his assistance in investigating some of the source material for this book. My previous legal secretary and longtime friend, Judy Payne, was also instrumental in conducting interviews and researching materials for a book on the history of the Medicine Mound community.

Another friend, Jeanene Stermer, serves as the manager of the Downtown Medicine Mound Museum, which is located in the Medicine Mound community south of Quanah, Texas. Jeanene has helped me research some of the stories and provided some of the pictures appearing in this book. Jimmy Clay, another longtime friend and professional artist, contributed artwork for this book as well as several of my previous books.

Finally, many thanks to my dear wife, Gayla, who, as usual, has done "the heavy lifting" as my secretary, my research assistant, and my editorial critic in writing this book.

To all of the above people, I offer my many, many thanks. It makes writing true stories about Western life of yesteryear an enjoyable trip through time.

Bill Neal
Abilene, Texas

ABOUT THE AUTHOR

Bill Neal, rancher, news reporter, lawyer, and author, grew up on a West Texas ranch and still owns and operates a ranch near Quanah, Texas. After college he began a career as a news reporter and then moved to law. He began his legal career as a briefing attorney for the Texas Supreme Court. Then he returned to his West Texas hometown and practiced criminal law for forty years—twenty as a district attorney and twenty in private practice doing criminal defense work.

When he retired in 2004, Neal began writing award-winning nonfiction tales of justice and injustice, beginning with *Getting Away with Murder on the Texas Frontier: Notorious Killings & Celebrated Trials* followed by *From Guns to Gavels: How Justice Grew Up in the Outlaw West*, both which won multiple awards. Neal has since written four books in the same genre. Here he presents a collection of interesting and sometimes funny stories from his life.

Bill and his wife, Gayla, live in Abilene, Texas.